Principles of Righteousness

Finney's Lessons on Romans
Volume I
Twenty-Fifth Anniversary Edition

C. G. Finney

Books by L.G. Parkhurst, Jr.

Finney's Systematic Theology:
New Expanded Edition
Compiled and edited from the works of Charles G. Finney
Minneapolis: Bethany House Publishers, 1994

Prayer Steps to Serenity: The Twelve Steps Journey:
New Serenity Prayer Edition
Edmond: Agion Press, 2006

Prayer Steps to Serenity:
Daily Quiet Time Edition
Edmond: Agion Press, 2005

How God Teaches Us to Pray:
Lessons from the Lives of Francis and Edith Schaeffer
Milton Keynes, England: Nelson Word Ltd. 1993

How to Pray in the Spirit
Compiled and edited from the works of John Bunyan
Grand Rapids: Kregel Publications, 1993, 1998

Principles of Prayer
Compiled and edited from the works of Charles Finney
Minneapolis: Bethany House Publishers, 1980, 2001

Answers to Prayer
Compiled and edited from the works of Charles Finney
Minneapolis: Bethany House Publishers, 1983, 2002

Principles of Devotion
Compiled and edited from the works of Charles Finney
Minneapolis: Bethany House Publishers, 1987

Principles of Righteousness

Finney's Lessons on Romans
Volume I

Charles Grandison Finney

With Commentary from Henry Cowles
The Longer Epistles of Paul

Compiled and Newly Edited for Today by
L.G. Parkhurst, Jr.

"For the kingdom of God is not a matter of eating and drinking, but of righteousness, peace and joy in the Holy Spirit."—Romans 14:17

Agion Press
AgionPress.com

Published by Agion Press, P.O. Box 1052, Edmond, OK 73083-1052

Cover Photo and Cover Design
Copyright © 2006 by Kathryn Winterscheidt: Used by Permission

The Charles G. Finney Lessons on Romans
      Volume I: *Principles of Righteousness*
      Volume II: *Principles of Peace*:
      Volume III: *Principles of Joy in the Holy Spirit*

Publisher's Cataloging-in-Publication Data

Finney, Charles Grandison, 1792-1875.
      Principles of Righteousness: Finney's Lessons on Romans, Volume I /
Charles G. Finney ; compiled and edited by Louis Gifford Parkhurst, Jr.
      207 p. : port. ; 23 cm.
      1, Bible. N.T. Romans—Sermons. 2. Sermons, American.
I. Parkhurst, Louis Gifford, 1946-   . II. Title
BS2665.4.F57   2006   227'.106
ISBN 0-9778053-0-1 (pbk.):   LCCN 2006922106
ISBN 0-9778053-1-X (e-book.):
P 10 9 8 7 6 5 4 3 2 1

Principles of Righteousness
Volume I

Preface

1. The Wrath of God Against Those Who Withstand His Truth
   Romans 1:18-19—1857 11
2. God's Wrath Against Those Who Withstand His Truth
   Romans 1:18-19—1858 23
3. Holding the Truth in Unrighteousness
   Romans 1:18-19—1861 35
4. On the Atonement
   Romans 3:25-26—1856 53
5. Sanctification by Faith
   Romans 3:31—1837 67
6. The Foundation, Conditions, Relations, and Results of Faith
   Romans 4:1-5—1850 79
7. The Rationality of Faith
   Romans 4:20-21—1851 93
8. God's Love Commended to Us
   Romans 5:8—1858 105
9. The Nature of Death to Sin
   Romans 6:7—1840 115
10. Death to Sin through Christ
    Romans 6:11—1853 125
11. Sanctification under Grace
    Romans 6:14—1839 141
12. The Wages of Sin
    Romans 6:23—1854 153
Study Questions for Individuals and Groups 171
Henry Cowles Commentary on Key Verses from Romans 185
About Agion Press 207

Principles of Peace
Volume II

Preface

1. Legal Experience
   Romans 7—1837
2. Christ the Husband of the Church
   Romans 7:4—1837
3. Revival of Sin and the Law
   Romans 7:9—1853
4. Thanks for the Gospel Victory
   Romans 7:25—1840
5. Justification
   Romans 8:1—1843
6. Total Depravity
   Romans 8:7—1836
7. Moral Depravity
   Romans 8:7—1862
8. License, Bondage and Liberty
   Romans 8:15—1854
9. Spirit of Prayer
   Romans 8:26-27—1835
10. All Things for Good to Those That Love God
    Romans 8:28—1847
11. All Events Ruinous to the Sinner
    Romans 8:28—1847
12. All Things for Good to Those That Love God
    Romans 8:28—1852
13. Religion of the Law and the Gospel
    Romans 9:30—1837
Study Questions for Individuals and Groups
Henry Cowles Commentary

Principles of Joy in the Holy Spirit
Volume III

Preface

1. Men, Ignorant of God's Righteousness Would Establish Own
   Romans 10:3—1855
2. The Way to be Holy
   Romans 10:4—1843
3. On Believing with the Heart
   Romans 10:10—1856
4. Conformity to the World
   Romans 12:2—1837
5. How to Prevent Our Employments from Injuring Our Souls
   Romans 12:11—1839
6. Being in Debt
   Romans 13:8—1839
7. Nature of True Virtue
   Romans 13:8-10—1843
8. Love Is the Whole of Religion
   Romans 13:10—1837
9. Love Worketh No Ill
   Romans 13:10—1841
10. Putting on Christ
    Romans 13:14—1843
11. The Kingdom of God in Consciousness
    Romans 14:17—1861
12. Total Abstinence A Christian Duty
    Romans 14:21—1850
13. Doubtful Actions are Sinful
    Romans 14:23—1837
Study Questions for Individuals and Groups
Henry Cowles Commentary

Charles Grandison Finney
Revivalist, Pastor, and Theologian
1792-1875

"*The writer is inclined to regard Charles G. Finney as the greatest evangelist and theologian since the days of the apostles. Over eighty-five in every hundred persons professing conversion to Christ in Finney's meetings remained true to God. Finney seems to have had the power of impressing the conscience with the necessity of holy living in such a manner as to procure the most lasting results.*"

From *Deeper Experiences of Famous Christians* by James Gilcrist Lawson, Anderson, Indiana: The Warner Press,1978, page 175.

Preface

Charles G. Finney's *Principles of Righteousness: Finney's Lessons on Romans,* Volume I, begins the new "Finney's Principles" series, which commenced twenty-five years ago with the first book in the series *Principles of Prayer*, published by Bethany House Publishers in 1980. No one knew at the time that Finney's lectures and sermons in this series would become immensely popular. Of course, many devoted Christians promoted Finney's teachings.

Finney's inspired preaching eventually led him to be named "America's Greatest Revivalist." He inspired Christians all around the world to live totally for Jesus Christ. Most of the revivals that followed Finney's successful endeavors relied either directly or indirectly on the principles and theology that Finney used and taught, especially in his *Lectures on Revivals of Religion*.

As I reflect on the past twenty-five years, many of the best teachers of Finney's revival theology have gone to be with the Lord. I think especially of those who tremendously helped me in my Christian walk, Harry Conn and Gordon Olson. The popularity and life-transforming teachings of Finney, promoted in so many effective ways by these two men and others, gave many the desire to read as many of the sermons and lectures by Finney as they could find. In turn, the Holy Spirit moved me to compile and edit the first "Finney's Principles" series. Though not a real part of that series, the last Charles Finney book that I helped compile and edit was *Finney's Systematic Theology*.

Agion Press revives the "Finney's Principles" series beginning with *Principles of Righteousness*, the first of three volumes of Finney's Lessons on the Apostle Paul's *Letter to the Romans*. To help more people study Finney today, I have newly edited *Finney's Lessons on Romans* for today's

Preface

reader. Also, in this new series, you will find Study Questions for Individuals and Groups in the back of the book, and the Commentary by Henry Cowles on the key verses that relate to *Finney's Lessons on Romans*. Agion Press has enlarged the type and the book size for easier reading, annotating, and study. The titles *Principles of Righteousness*, *Principles of Peace*, and *Principles of Joy in the Holy Spirit* come from the theme of Romans 14:17, "For the kingdom of God is not a matter of eating and drinking, but of righteousness, peace and joy in the Holy Spirit." Study guides, notebooks, and additional free resources are available on the "Finney's Principles" website at FinneysPrinciples.org.

I do wish to thank my family for loving and helping me in many ways over the years as I have served as a pastor and have studied Finney's works. Once again, Kathryn Winterscheidt has created a beautiful book cover, as she did for my *Prayer Steps to Serenity: The Twelve Step Journey* and the new *Prayer Steps to Serenity: Daily Quiet Time Edition*. All the love, praise, and thanksgiving goes to Jesus Christ, my Lord and Savior, in whose Kingdom I am honored and blessed to serve.

Love in the Lamb of God
L.G. Parkhurst, Jr..
November 30, 2005

1

The Wrath of God Against Those Who Withstand His Truth

1857

For the wrath of God is revealed from heaven against all ungodliness and unrighteousness of men, who hold the truth in unrighteousness; Because that which may be known of God is manifest in them; for God hath showed it unto them.—Romans 1:18-19—KJV

The wrath of God is being revealed from heaven against all the godlessness and wickedness of men who suppress the truth by their wickedness, since what may be known about God is plain to them, because God has made it plain to them.—Romans 1:18-19—NIV

The context shows that in these words the apostle has his eye especially on those who, not having a written revelation from God, might yet know Him in His works of nature. Paul's view is that God's invisible attributes are apparent to the human mind. Since the creation of our world, God has revealed His attributes by the things He has made. In and by means of His works, we may learn of His eternal power

11

and His real divinity. Hence, everyone has some means of knowing the great truths that pertain to God, our infinite Creator. Therefore, God may justly hold people responsible for accepting this truth reverently, and rendering to their Creator the homage due Him. They are utterly without excuse if they withhold the honor God deserves to receive from them.

What is the true idea of unrighteousness?

Unrighteousness cannot be less than the negation of righteousness, and may imply more or less of positive wickedness. Here the question will arise—what is righteousness? To which I answer, rightness—moral rightness. Originally, the term was used in regard to material things to denote what is straight, for example, a straight line. Unrighteousness, the opposite of this, must mean what is morally crooked, distorted—not in harmony with the rightness of God's law. To denote sin, the scriptures employ some terms which properly signify a negation, or utter absence of what should be. Some theologians have maintained that the true idea of sin is simply negative, supposing sin to consist in not doing and not being what one ought to do and to be. This idea is strongly implied in our text. Sin is, indeed, a neglect to do known duty and a refusal to comply with known obligation. Inasmuch as love is required always and of all people, sin must be a state of real disobedience. Suffice it then to say that unrighteousness is an omission—a known omission—a refusal to be what we should be, and to do what we should do. Of course, it is only and wholly voluntary. The mind's refusal to obey God is a matter of its own free choice.

What is "holding the truth in unrighteousness"?

The original definition of "hold" means to hold back, to restrain. The idea here is that a person restrains the legitimate influence of the truth and will not let it have its proper sway over his will.

God so constituted the human mind that truth is its natural stimulus. The stimulus of truth, if the truth is not restrained and held back, would lead the mind naturally to obey God. A person holds back the truth through his own unrighteousness when for selfish reasons he over-rules and restrains its natural influence and will not allow the truth to take possession and hold sway over his mind.

What is "the wrath of God revealed from heaven"?

God, manifesting himself from heaven, has revealed His high and just displeasure against all restraining of the truth and withstanding of its influence. Before I proceed to show *why* God reveals His wrath from heaven, I must come very near to some of you and talk to you in great frankness and faithfulness. I do not charge on you that you have been outwardly immoral, but you have restrained the truth, you have with-stood its influence. Therefore, you are the very persons against whom God reveals His wrath. This is true of everyone who has not given himself up to the influence of truth. You have restrained the natural influence of truth; therefore, God has revealed His wrath against you.

This is a terrible thing. The wrath of a king is terrible. How much more so is the wrath of God! Who can stand before Him when once He shall arise in His wrath to avenge His truth and His own glorious name!

Why does God's wrath wax hot against this sin?

Comprehensively the reason is this: "Withstanding the truth is resist-ing God's revealed claims of love and obedience and is therefore the whole of sin." When you withhold the truth, you compromise everything. This is the very essence—the true idea of sin. Sin is deliberate, intelligent, and intentional rebellion against God. There could be no obligation until your conscience affirms it to you. The conscience cannot affirm obliga-tion until some knowledge of God is revealed to your mind. When this knowledge of God is revealed, then conscience must and will affirm obli-gation. After this, the more conscience is developed, the more it unfolds, the more strongly it affirms your obligation to obey God.

Suppose a person were created asleep. Until he awakes, there could be in his mind no knowledge of God—not one idea of God; consequently no sense of obligation to obey God. As soon as the moral functions of

1

Romans 1:18-19

the reason and the conscience create a sense of obligation, then the mind must make a decision. It must choose either to obey or to disobey God. It must elect either to take God's law as its rule of duty or reject it.

The alternative of rejecting God makes it necessary to hold back the truth and withstand its claims. We might almost say that these processes are substantially identical—resisting the natural influence of God's truth on the mind, and withstanding the known claims of God. When you know the truth concerning God, the great question becomes whether or not you will obey it. If your heart says "No," you do of course resist the claims of truth. You hold it back through your own unrighteousness.

The very apprehending of moral truth concerning God renders it impossible to be indifferent. Once seeing God's claims, you cannot avoid acting upon them one way or the other. After you know your duty, to stop and hold your mind aloof from obedience is being just as wicked as you can be. You disown your whole obligation toward God, and practically say unto God, "Depart from me, for I desire not the knowledge of Your ways." Is not this as wicked as you can be, with the light you may have at the time? What thing could you do more wicked?

Look at this matter a little further. Holding back the truth through unrighteousness implies the total rejection of the moral law as a rule of duty. This must be the case, because when light or understanding concerning the meaning of this law comes before this person, he repels it and resists its claims, thus virtually saying, "That law is no rule of duty to me." Thus resisting the influence of truth, he practically denies all obligations to God. Truth coming before his mind, he perceives his obligation, but he withholds his mind from its sway.

You may have observed that some people seem to have no sense of any other obligation except that created by human law. Legal obligation can reach them, but not moral. They will not pay an honest debt unless it is in such a shape that the strong hand of the law can take hold of them. Others have no sensibility to any claims except those that serve their business reputation. Take away their fear of losing their reputation; remove all the inducements to do right except those that pertain to moral obligation, and see if they will ever do what is right. In a practical sense, they reject and deny God's rights altogether, and equally so, their own obligations to

God. Their conduct, put into words, would read, "I have some respect for human law and some fear of human penalty; but, for God's law or penalty I care nothing!" It is easy to see that to hold back the truth in this manner is the perfection of wickedness. Suppose a person refrains from sinning *only* because of his obligations to human laws: he shows that he fears human penalties only and has no fear of God.

Holding the truth in unrighteousness settles all questions regarding a person's moral character. You may know the person with unerring certainty. He has taken his position. His course is fixed. As to moral obligation, he cares nothing. The fact is this: perceived moral obligation does not influence his actions at all. He has become totally dishonest. This settles the question of his character. Until he reveres God's authority, there is not a particle of moral goodness in him. He does not act with even common honesty. His moral character toward God is formed and is easily known. If he had any moral honesty, the perceived fact of his own moral obligation would influence his mind; but we see it does not at all. He shuts down the gate on all the claims of truth and will not allow them to sway his will; hence, it must be that his heart is fully committed to wickedness.

God reveals His wrath from heaven against all who hold back the truth because this attitude of the will shows that they are reckless of their obligations toward God. It shows that a moral claim on their heart and conscience goes for nothing. If you restrain the truth from influencing your mind, this very fact proves that you do not mean to serve God. Some of you know that you are not doing what you know to be your duty. You are conscious that the presence of known duty does not move you. You have not done one act of obedience to God's claims *because* they are God's claims.

Not only does this settle the question of moral character—which is of itself a good reason for God's wrath—but it also settles the question of moral relations. Because it shows that your moral character is altogether corrupt and wrong, it also shows that with regard to moral relations, you are really God's enemy. From the moment you resist the claims of moral truth, God must regard you as His enemy, and not by any means as His obedient subject. Not in any figurative sense, but in its most literal sense, you are God's enemy; therefore, God must be highly displeased with you. If He were not, His own conscience would condemn Him. You must know that it must be His duty to reveal to you His displeasure. Since He must feel it, He ought to be open and honest with you. You could not, with good reason, wish God to be otherwise. All of you who know moral truth, yet do not obey it—who admit obligation which yet you refuse to obey—you are the people who hold the truth in unrighteousness. Settle this in your minds—if you restrain the influence of any truth known concerning God and your duty, then against you is His wrath revealed from heaven.

Wherein and how is God's wrath revealed?

Perhaps you are already asking yourself this question. Moralists are prone to make it and to say, "We do not see any wrath coming. If we are as good as those who profess to be Christians, why shall we not be saved as well as they?" Therefore, how does God reveal His wrath against this great wickedness?

By conscience. Your conscience affirms that God must be displeased with you. It certifies to you beforehand that you are guilty and that God cannot accept you.

By remorse. Remorse, which sometimes affects sinners, confirms even more God's displeasure. True, the feeling of remorse belongs to the sensibility or feelings; never the less, remorse does give admonitory warning. Its voice must be accounted as the voice of God in the human soul. God, who made that sensibility so that it will sometimes recoil under a sense of guilt and turn back to consume the life and joy of the soul, did not make it to lie. It is strange that anyone should suppose remorse to be itself the punishment threatened of God against sin and the whole of it. Far from it! Remorse is not that punishment which God has threatened; it is only a premonition of it.

By fear. The very fears people feel are often to be taken as an indication that the thing they dread is a reality. Why is it that people in their sins are so often greatly afraid to die? It is no other than a trumpet-tone of the voice of God sounding up from the depths of their very nature. How can they overlook the fact that these grim forebodings of coming doom are indeed a revelation of wrath made in the very nature God has given them!

By judicial abandonment. Another revelation of God's wrath is His judicial abandonment of sinners. God manifests His despair of doing anything more for their salvation when He manifestly withdraws His Spirit and gives them over to hopeless abandonment. Withdrawing His Spirit, God leaves them in great moral blindness. They may have been able to see and to discriminate spiritual things somewhat before. But after God forsakes them, they seem almost utterly void of this power. Everything is dark; all is confused. Once the light of the Holy Spirit is withdrawn, it is practically vain for the sinner himself or for his sympathizing friends to expect his salvation. This mental darkness over all spiritual things is God's curse on his rejection of truth and significantly forebodes his speedy doom.

By moral paralysis. Analogous to judicial abandonment is the indication given in a moral paralysis of the conscience. Strangely, it seems to have lost its sensibility; its ready ability of moral discrimination is gone. Its perceptions seem unaccountably obtuse, and the tone of its voice waxes feeble and almost inaudible. Practically speaking, one might almost as well have no conscience at all. What does this paralysis of conscience indicate? Plainly, that God has abandoned that soul. The conscience, so long over-borne by a perverse will, gives way; and God ceases to sustain its vitality any longer.

It is painful to see how people in this condition of judicial abandonment and paralysis of conscience strain their endeavors when such debility comes down upon them. They become indifferent and diverting influences are so potent that they drop their endeavors, powerless. Once, their conscience had some activity. Truth fell on their mind with appreciable force, and they were aware of resisting it. However, by and by, a state of moral feeling resulted in which their mind was no longer conscious of refusing; indeed, it seems scarcely conscious of anything whatever. The person has restrained the influence of truth until conscience has mainly suspended its function. Like the drunkard who has lost all perception of the moral wrong of intemperance, and who has brought this insensibility on himself by incessant violations of his better judgment, so the sinner has refused to hear the truth, until the truth now refuses to move him. What is the meaning of this strange phenomenon? It is one of the ways in which God reveals His indignation at a person's great wickedness.

Consider this case: an ungodly student, put on the intellectual race-course alongside of his classmates, soon becomes ambitious and jealous. At first, he will probably have some sense of this sin; however, he soon loses this sense and passes on as if unconscious of any sin. What is this but a revelation of God's displeasure?

By direct punishment. The wrath of God against those who hold back the truth in unrighteousness is abundantly revealed in the Bible. Think of what Jesus Christ said to the hypocritical Scribes and Pharisees: "Fill ye up then the measure of your fathers" (Matthew 23:32—KJV). What did Jesus mean by that? Their fathers had filled their cup of sin until God could bear with them no longer. Then He filled up His cup of wrath and poured it forth on the nation and there was no remedy. Christ intimates that this shall be with the Scribes and Pharisees. What is this but to reveal His wrath against them for holding back the truth through unrighteousness?

By strong delusion. God lets such sinners die in their sins. Observe how, step-by-step, God gave them one revelation after another of His wrath against their sin—remorse, moral blindness, decay of moral sensibility, and the plain assertions of His word. All these failing, He gives them up to some strong delusion that they may believe a lie. God himself says, "For this cause God shall send them strong delusion, that they should believe a lie: that they all might be damned who believed not the truth, but had pleasure in unrighteousness" (2 Thessalonians 2:11, 12—KJV). It is painfully instructive to study the workings of modern delusions, especially spiritualism—to notice how it has come in following the track of those great revivals that blessed our country a few years ago. I know scores of people who passed through those revivals unblessed, and now they are mad with this delusion. They saw the glory of God in those scenes of revival power; but they turned away, and now they are mad on their idols, and crazy under their delusions. Having rejected the blessed Holy Spirit, they now follow deceiving spirits. God's word declares, "evil men and seducers shall wax worse and worse, deceiving, and being deceived" (2 Timothy 3:13—KJV). "Furthermore, since they did not think it worthwhile to retain the knowledge of God, he gave them over to a depraved mind, to do what ought not to be done" (Romans 1:28—NIV). God has given them up to die in their sins, and it will be an awful death! Draw near them gently, and ask a few kind questions. You will soon see that they make no just moral discriminations. All is dark which needs to be light, before they can see and find the gate of life.

REMARKS

You may notice the exact difference between saints and sinners, including among sinners all who profess Christianity who are not in an obedient state of mind. The exact difference is this: saints have adopted Gods' will as their law of activity, the rule that shall govern all their life and all their heart. You reveal God's will to them—this settles all further controversy. The very opposite of this is true of the sinner. With the sinner, the fact of God's supposed will has no such influence at all; usually no influence of any sort, unless it be to excite his opposition. Again, the true Christian, instead of restraining the influence of truth, acts up to his convictions. If the question of oughtness is settled, all is settled.

Suppose I say to a Christian, "I want you to do a certain thing. I think you must give so much of your money to this object." Then he replies, "I don't know about that, my money costs me great labor and pains." But I resume and say, "Let us look calmly at this question." And then I proceed to show him that the thing I ask of him is beyond a doubt his duty to God and to others. He interposes at once, "You need not say another word; that is enough. If it is my duty to Christ and to His people, I ask no more."

The sinner is not moved in this way. He knows his duty beforehand, but he has long disregarded its claims on him. You must appeal to his selfish interests if you would reach his heart. With the Christian, you need not appeal to his hopes or his fears. You only need to show him his duty to God. The sinner you can hope to move only by appeals to his self-interests. The reason for this is that his adopted course of life is to serve his

1

Romans 1:18-19

19

own interests, nothing higher.

With sinners, the question of religion is one of loss and gain. With Christians, it is only a question of right and duty toward God. This makes truth to the Christian important and duty imperative. But the sinner only asks. "What shall I gain? Or what shall I lose?" It is wholly a question of reward or danger. Indeed, so true is this that ministers often assume that the only availing motive with a sinner must be an appeal to his hopes and fears. They have mostly dropped out the consideration of right as between the sinner and God. They seem to have forgotten that in so far as they stop short of the idea of right and appeal only to the sinner's selfishness, their influence tends to make spurious converts.

If people enter upon the Christian life only for gain in the line of their hopes and fears, you must keep up the influence of these considerations and must expect to work upon these only. That is, you must expect to have selfish "Christians" and a selfish church. If you say to them, "This is your duty," they will reply, "What have we ever cared for duty? We were never converted to the doctrine of doing our duty. We became Christians, only for the sake of promoting our own interests, and we have nothing to do in the Christian life on any other motive." Now observe, they may modify this language a little if it seems too repugnant to the general convictions of decent people; nevertheless, this is their real meaning. They modify its language only on the same general principle of making everything subservient to self.

We see how great a mistake selfish "Christians" make when they say, "Am I not honest toward others? And is this not a proof of my piety?" What do you mean by "honest?" Are you honest toward God? Do you regard God's rights as much as you wish God to regard yours? Perhaps you ask, as many do. "What is my crime?" I answer, "Is it not enough for you to do nothing—really nothing—toward obedience to God? Is it not something serious that you refuse to do God's will and hold back the claims of His truth? What is the use of talking about your morality while you disregard the greatest of all moral claims and obligations—those that bind you to love and obey God? What can it avail you to say perpetually—Am I not moral and decent toward others?"

Sinner, if you think you are almost as good as Christians; in fact, it is much nearer the truth to say that you are almost as bad as devils! Indeed, you are fully as bad, except that you do not know as much as devils; therefore, you cannot be as wicked. You say. "We are kind to each other." So are devils. Their common purpose to war against God compels them to act in unity. They went together into the man possessed with a legion of devils, as we learn in the gospel history (see Mark 5:1-20). Very likely they are as kind toward each other in their league against God and goodness as you are toward your neighbors. Selfish people have little reason to compliment themselves on being kind and good to each other, while they withstand God. In these respects, sinners are only like devils in hell.

Now, my impenitent hearers—what do you say? Putting your conduct toward God into plain language, it would run thus: "You, Lord, call on me to repent. I shall refuse. You strive to enforce my obligation to repent by various truths. I hold back those truths from their legitimate influence on my mind. You insist on my submission to your authority. I shall do no such thing." This is only translating your current life and bearing toward God into plain words. If you were really to lift your face toward heaven and utter these words, it would be blasphemy. What do you think of it now? Do you not admit and often assert that actions speak louder than words? Do they not also speak more truthfully?

To those of you in business, let me make this appeal. What would you think of people who treated you as you treat God? You take your account to your customer and say, "Your account has been lying a long time past due. Will you be so good as to settle it? You cannot deny that it is a fair account of value received, and I understand you have abundant means to pay it." Suppose he very coldly refuses. You suggest the propriety of his giving some reasons for this refusal, and he tells you it is a fine time to get bigger interest on his money; therefore, he finds it more profitable to loan it out than to pay his debts. That is all. He is only selfish. All there is of it is simply this, that he cares for his own interests supremely, and cares little or nothing for yours when the two classes of interests—his and yours—come into competition. When you treat God as well as you want your creditors to treat you, you may hold up your head, as far as this goes, as an honest man. But as long as you do the very thing toward God which you condemn as infinitely selfish and mean from others toward you, you have little ground for self-complacent pride.

All this would be true and forcible even if God were no greater, no better, and had no higher and no more sacred rights than your own. How much more then are they weighty beyond expression, by how much God is greater, better, and holier than mortals!*

---

* Charles G. Finney, "The Oberlin Evangelist," December 9, 1857, *Sermons on the Way of Salvation*, 187–202, *Principles of Victory*, 30–37. For Review: Answer the Study Questions on page 171. For further study, read the Henry Cowles Commentary on the scripture text from Romans that relates to *Finney's Lessons on Romans*, Cowles Commentary is included in the back of this book and begins on page 184.

Editor's Note: To assist your study, I have included some scripture quotations that use the word "righteousness" from the Psalms, Proverbs, and Jesus on the following pages in this book: 66, 104, 124, 140, 152,170. Rather than just include blank even numbered pages when I wanted the new chapter page to begin on the right hand (odd numbered) page, I chose to add these Bible verses in these locations. One way to discover the Bible's meaning of a word is to study how the Bible uses that word, in context, in several locations in the Bible. I hope these verses expand your Biblical understanding of the word "righteousness."

2

God's Wrath Against Those Who Withstand His Truth

1858

For the wrath of God is revealed from heaven against all ungodliness and unrighteousness of men, who hold the truth in unrighteousness; Because that which may be known of God is manifest in them; for God hath showed it unto them. —Romans 1:18-19—KJV

The wrath of God is being revealed from heaven against all the godlessness and wickedness of men who suppress the truth by their wickedness, since what may be known about God is plain to them, because God has made it plain to them. —Romans 1:18-19—NIV

Every word of this impressive passage demands attentive consideration. It would seem that there is no end to its pointed and pungent applications to our practical life. We need to know how to interpret and apply these verses to our lives; for, as Paul wrote elsewhere, "Be not deceived; God is not mocked: for whatsoever a man soweth, that shall he also reap " (Galatians 6:7—KJV).

What is meant in our text by "hold" the truth?

We sometimes use "hold" or "holding" to signify holding fast to an opinion—having certain views as one's own. In this text, both the original word and the context concur to give another sense. To make this clear, I must first observe that truth is the natural stimulus to action. Its natural influence is to lead people to act. It will always have this tendency unless restrained. The word which Paul used here means precisely to restrain—to hold back the truth from exerting its appropriate influence. Paul assumes that the people of whom he speaks refuse to comply with the truth—this being the way in which people hold back the truth.

What is it to hold the truth "in unrighteousness"?

The meaning is not often well understood; therefore, you should carefully consider it. The original word for unrighteousness implies deficiency—a lack of righteousness. To hold the truth in unrighteousness implies that you see your duty, but you fail to do it. You restrain the truth so that it does not lead you on to do righteousness.

To illustrate this point, suppose some of you in business have claims against one of your neighbors. You have sold him goods on time. The day of payment has come and you need your payment. Your neighbor knows he ought to meet his promises promptly. You call on him. He acknowledges his obligation and says he knows he ought to pay you, but he fails to do it. In truth, he wants to speculate on his money. He can put it out at fifty per cent, and this, he thinks, is much better for him than paying his honest debts. What should you think if, when you call on him, and ask him if he ought not to pay, he should laugh you in the face? Indeed, says he, "Do you suppose I care what I ought to do?" He scoffs at the idea of moral obligation. Could you find words strong enough to paint his vileness? Yet the whole of it is—lack of righteousness—the lack of moral integrity, unrighteousness. Sinners do this toward God when they say to Him, "I know I ought to love and serve You, but what do I care for that? What is that to me? I have my own goals to achieve, and I can enjoy myself better in my own ways than in Your's." This language is not too strong. It does not at all exaggerate the infinite vileness of sinners who practically say, "I know God requires it, and I know it is right; but what of that?"

What shall we understand by "the wrath of God"?

Not any selfish anger, for God has none, and never can have. The wrath of God is a benevolent displeasure, such as a holy and good being must feel toward a wrong so monstrous. Would you not be greatly displeased with such conduct toward yourself? If a person honestly owed you, and yet was reckless of his obligation toward you, would you not think his conduct an outrage? Would you not be greatly displeased? Would you not feel deeply that you have reason for the displeasure you feel? Certainly, and by how much the more holy you are, by so much the more deeply and surely will you be displeased.

How is the wrath of God revealed?

By convictions. Partly, the wrath of God is revealed in the irresistible convictions of our own minds. We cannot but believe that God is displeased with us for holding back the truth through our unrighteousness. We know this as a first truth of reason, and cannot but know it. It is thus revealed to us in the strongest possible manner. Our necessary conceptions of God are such that it is impossible for us to deny that God is and must be displeased with this sin.

By providence. Moreover, the Bible reveals this often, I might say—everywhere. God's providence reveals it. For committing this sin, we know that we deserve to be damned and sent to hell forthwith, yet we are not; God lets us live yet longer. It is plain that God arranged many things in His providence for the purpose of reforming us. Hence, it is apparent, even from the revelations God makes of His providence, that He is disposed to forgive. Some have said that we never could infer God's mercy on grounds of natural theology; from His external providences apart from His written revelation. Yet, who does not know that all people have an idea of hope—and of themselves as "prisoners of hope"—the question of their doom being not already settled as it would be if they were now in hell.

By punishment. The Bible has settled this question. The original condition of being saved, which was perfect obedience, has given place to another system in which people having sinned are offered pardon—a system which while it shows that God does indeed hate sin, yet shows also that He has mercy in His heart and longs to exercise it toward the guilty sinner. Hence, all along through the past history of our world, God has come forth ever and anon to reveal His indignation against sin, as in the deluge on the old world; on Sodom, Egypt and rebellious Israel. Notice how, all down the history of human sinning, God has come forth in flashes of glory and of power, terrible to human hearts! In every way practicable to a system of probation and of mercy, God has revealed His wrath against sin.

By prophetic remorse. God reveals His wrath also in that prophetic remorse which brings agony to the soul of the sinner and forewarns him of the coming wrath of his God. Sinners are afraid to die. Why are they afraid to die rather than live? Because sinners know they are sinners, and they dread to meet an offended God. This dread is prophetic.

By judicial blindness. God's wrath is revealed moreover in the judicial blindness to which God gives up sinners when they have abused His truth too long. We see this in the gloomy death-bed; in the dark despair under which sinners die. Alas for him! Everywhere along his dark way to hell, God flashes terror and wrath! Behind all these displays of love and mercy, you may hear the mutterings of offended justice. The flashes of His sword gleam out, revealing His wrath against all unrighteousness.

What do "ungodliness" and "unrighteousness" mean?

Our text says, "God's wrath is revealed against all ungodliness and unrighteousness." What does "ungodliness" mean? Ungodliness is the absence of piety toward God. The original word is a compound of two; one of which gives us the idea of worship and reverence for God, and the other indicates the utter absence and lack of this. Therefore, ungodliness means no worship—no regard for God—no recognition of His goodness or greatness. God comes before the sinner, a glorious object of love and worship, but the sinner refuses to regard Him. Indeed, he has no family alter, no closet! Learn this terrible lesson! God reveals His wrath against all withholding of love and worship, praise and adoration. See some of those who think they are moral, but they never worship God, never love Him—never acknowledge Him in any of their ways! Take notice! Do you hear what God says? Behind of all this sweet flowing of mercy, you may hear the mutterings of Jehovah's thunder; His wrath against all ungodliness and unrighteousness! If you do not worship, love, and obey God, you are an ungodly sinner, and God reveals His awful wrath against you!

Unrighteousness seems to refer to neglect of duty toward others; refusing to pay one's honest debts, refusing to meet any honorable obligations. Any neglect of duty to others is unrighteousness. The word means shortcomings. Perhaps no other term translates it so perfectly. It embraces all falling short of duty. This is always voluntary and blameworthy; just as you always regard it when you charge someone who owes you with shortcoming and wrong if he can pay you, but will not. This guilt is at the door of all who admit that they ought to love God and serve Him, but will not. All you who withhold from God or others what is due from you; all you who allow yourselves to live below your own standard, on you, God's wrath must fall. If you allow yourself to live in voluntary neglect of your duty, against you is God's wrath revealed. If you find fault with others for neglect of duty, you show in this that you know your own duty and are therefore in the greater sin. It is very common for sinners to do this toward Christians, to tattle on those who profess Christianity as hypocrites and sinners. So are you, and all the more so because of the clearness with which you can discern the shortcomings of others. All you who hold one thing in theory and another in practice, who know the right yet choose to do the wrong, what else can be said of you except that you hold back the truth in unrighteousness? Some complain of their coldness and make many confessions, yet they fail just as much again in their duties. They are like the person who talks well about paying his honest debts, who never fails to admit his obligations, but always fails to pay. He can pay but will not! If this happened to you, you would surely cry out, "What a villain !" Yet this

2

Romans 1:18-19

case scarcely begins to portray the guilt of the sinner against God! Who of you have this moral attitude toward your Maker? Will you pause and ask "Who"?

Why does God declare His wrath against these sins?

Holding back or suppressing the truth implies you know the truth. People could not hold back the truth if they did not know it. Holding back the truth also implies the ability to obey it; otherwise, people could not be denounced for holding it back and for refusing to obey it. How differently do the scriptures speak on this point from many theologians! Some theologians are prone to say that no mere man can obey God's law. The Bible says no such thing. Speaking with special reference to those who had not even a written law, Paul teaches that they knew enough of God to obey and had ample power to obey. People, hearing the truth concerning their duty, are not passive—they cannot be. By their very nature, they must have this power to feel its force, and feeling it, to yield or to resist. The text implies a positive effort to resist the truth—to rule down its demands. To take deliberately the opposite course to that required is no accidental thing. It is a direct refusal to fulfill our acknowledged obligations to God. This amounts virtually to the denial of all moral obligation and accountability. It is a direct rejection of God's authority. The sinner decides the great question whether God's will shall be law to him by answering, "No." Neither God, nor His law, nor the sinner's own sense of duty shall be his rule. For the sinner to disregard the known claims of God's revealed truth is nothing less than to decide fairly, openly, to the very face of God, that he will not obey Him. Knowing God's will, he says, is not a reason that shall influence him.

Remember, holding the truth in unrighteousness implies that there is no inability to obey it. For if there were such inability, God's wrath could not go forth against the sinner. How very different is this from that theology which represents God's commands as so hard that people, who are very well disposed to do the best they can, cannot obey them!

A good reason for such strong language against this disobedience is the sinner's total dishonesty; his determination to perform no duty to God. It is a full rejection of God's claims. It virtually says to God, "I don't care for You. Say what You will, what do I care? I know Your commandments are right, but I shall withhold my heart. I will not acknowledge God!" Surely, this is the very essence of all iniquity; the sum of all villainy. What would you think if anybody should serve you so? You would feel that he greatly wronged you—that those who treated you so had not the least particle of moral honesty! If a man should treat you in just this way, and then set up the claim of being fair minded and honorable, what would you say? You would say that so far from being right-minded, he looks with perfect contempt on the idea of moral obligation! It shall not bind him!

To be sure, a dishonest person may pay his debts at the bank rather than ruin his credit and be denied more money. But suppose you could not reach him with the sense of moral obligation; then, would you not say, "He is the perfection of a villain!" This language is not too strong. There is no crime the person would not commit if it were convenient and he thought it would achieve his selfish interests. Who could trust him? There is no crime on earth or in hell that he would refrain from committing on the score of moral obligation. Why? Because moral obligation does not touch him; he has discarded its claims.

Now, what do you say? Is it amazing to you that God should speak thus against this sin of all sins? Against the one who says, "I do not care for God! Let Him say what He will and do what He will, I care not for my obligations to obey Him!"

There is still another point of view from which to contemplate this sin. Not only does this sinner not care for God; he cares nothing for the universal good. God has bidden him to care for the good of others, to love his neighbor as himself. God has placed before the sinner His own example and thus seeks to lead him on in real benevolence. But this sinner will do no such thing. Whereas God's whole law as to our fellow human beings is condensed into this one precept: "You shall love your neighbor as yourself," the sinner applies to God the same doctrine which Chief Justice Taney unjustly applies to black men in their relation to white. Taney said, "Black men have no rights which white men are bound to respect." The sinner says, "God has no rights that I am bound to respect. And if God asks me to respect the rights of others, I will not do it for His sake!"

2

Romans 1:18-19

This state of mind and heart is total depravity! A man repudiating all moral obligation—going, as to God, into universal repudiation—a known, willful, repudiation of all moral obligation and nothing less!

And this is by no means a caricature. God tries to get your sympathy and to draw you into fellowship with himself in loving His great family. But you say, "No! Let me have no fellowship with God, or with the good among His creatures!"

Now, ought not God be displeased with you? Could you respect Him if He were not displeased with the unrighteous and ungodly? Surely, you would say, "He is not fit to govern the universe! Nay, He is worse than the sinner, since He knows infinitely more."

Now, I put this to your conscience, could you exonerate God from great blame if He were to be indifferent to such a sin as this of disowning moral obligation? Remember, I am not speaking now of open vice, in itself intrinsically hateful and disgusting; but of declining to obey—of falling short of duty. What would you think of your children if they were to do just that thing toward you; uniformly fail and refuse to obey your commands or respect their obligations to you?

Since God feels this way, it behooves Him to express it. What else than this could God reasonably do? Of the wicked God says, "Whose judgment now of a long time lingereth not, and their damnation slumbereth not" (2 Peter 2:3—KJV). You may hear it rolling like distant thunder. O! How terrible when it shall break forth in one eternal storm!

Long time Mercy has been holding back the uplifted arm of Justice, while God's heart has been heaving with holy indignation—so long that you are even thinking God will never arise to vengeance. "You thought I was altogether such a one as yourself, but I will reprove you and I will set you in order before your eyes."

REMARKS

Withstanding God's truth is the very essence of all wickedness, because it is the mind resisting the truth and refusing obedience to it when most pressed to obey. It involves the utmost dishonesty. It is withholding your good will from the universe.

Did you ever think of this when you refuse to work for God and to feel with Him for the good of the universe; what if your refusal really frustrated His benevolent plans? What then? Would not that be an infinite mischief, an untold calamity? But if you refuse to work with God, if you set yourself against God's plans, no thanks to you that your course does not frustrate all God's benevolence toward the universe! So far as you can do it, it is done. When you hold the truth in unrighteousness, you have the responsibility of doing all you can to make the universe infinitely wretched, both God and all His creatures.

You think it would be mean of God to shut you out of heaven, to say to you, as He did to the rich man, "Son, remember that you in your life time received your good things, and there are no more for you!" (see Luke 16:19-31). Why should not God do this? You do not love God's happiness nor that of others. You flatly disown all your obligations to do either. You refuse to seek your neighbor's good; no thanks to you if he does not lie down in everlasting sorrow.

In holding back the truth, you set the worst example possible, for more people lose their souls by neglect than by open vice. To set them this example is to tempt them in their weakest, most susceptible point.

The more enlightened people are, the greater is their guilt. Sometimes I have had such views of the sins of many here in this matter that I cannot think of preaching anything else. Some say, "No place like Oberlin—such Sabbaths, such Christian privileges!" Yet for all this, it may be the wickedest place on earth, just because it is so highly favored of God with gospel light.

The Jews thought there was nothing like their beloved city: "beautiful for situation, the joy of the whole earth;" yet how terribly did God pour out the vials of His wrath even on that once holy city (see Psalms 48:2)! He punished them as He rarely ever punished any other nation. Many of those who often bless themselves for their morality and for their gospel privileges never measure the guilt of knowing their duty, yet choosing not to do it! They are like those who will not pay their debts, yet boast of being very moral and civil. Hear them boast: "We do nothing very bad. To be sure, we never mean to pay our debts, but we are not openly vicious." What would you say of such hypocrites? More than once, when I have

31

attended meetings and have heard Christians confess their backslidings, I have asked, "Do you mean to defend that? Do you intend to go on living so?" It is awful to hear people say, "We know our duty, but we do not do it." Especially so, when they make great professions also, and insist that they hope in Christ. How shocking to hear one confess, as I once heard a man, "Lord, we have sinned against You all this day, and we expect to sin against You all day tomorrow. O Lord, forgive us!" What does this mean? Does he assume that he cannot help it? If this is true, why does God condemn people for holding the truth in unrighteousness? I know very well that he could have said, "O, I do as well as I can." If that is true, why does he confess that he is not doing as well as he can; that is, why does he confess his sin? Can God respect those who say they are sinning all the time when they do not believe it to be so?

On this point, people stop their self-examination where they should not. They ought to pursue their self-examination until they ascertain what sin is and is not. For example, your neighbor says, "You owe me." You reply. "Perhaps not. Let us see." You go on and examine until you find how the case is. So you should. So you should do toward God. But suppose you find that you owe your neighbor, and then you stop there and refuse to pay. That is the most provoking place to stop—the whole question of debt and consequently of duty, being settled, but nothing more done. This is the way many treat God—the way they shamefully abuse Him!

O. sinner! Never more complain of others for not fulfilling their obligations to you while you deny yours to God! Say to yourself, "It will be soon enough for me to complain of any creature in the universe when I have ceased to repudiate my obligations to God! How can I stand before this appalling fact! Certainly I know I ought to be treated as the universal enemy of God and all the good."

Indeed, if the sinner's eyes were open, he would see God's awful wrath kindling up ready to burst upon his guilty head. Backslider, is it you? How old is your love? You who once plighted your faith and gave to God your right hand, where are you? Have you gone back to sin and shame? God calling after you, and you fleeing. What shall God say to you? Even now His voice rings in your ear, "Return, O backsliding daughter, for I am married to you" (see Jeremiah 3:14; 49:4, and the prophet Hosea). And where are you? Gone after other lovers! O shame! What can be more dishonorable—more shameful!

You can see why many people seem to grow more and more hardened in sin. They take no action under the pressure of truth upon their heart and conscience. Is it any wonder that the wrath of God is revealed from heaven against all such sinners? Think now, will you do the very same thing again today? Will you practically say, "I know my duty, but I will not do it." You recollect that Pollock represents the sinner wailing in hell, as hearing continually an echoing response to his agonizing groans: "You knew your duty, but you did it not." This, O sinner, must be the answer forever to all your wailings of sorrow in the world of woe. Sometimes the image of someone, once a dear friend on earth, will come up before my mind as he drinks of the cup of everlasting woe, and I see him fleeing to escape, but the waves of damnation follow hard after him and he is overwhelmed before them! Alas, that he did not yield his soul to the claims of truth when he might! I have not often preached on the subject of God's eternal wrath against sinners. Perhaps I have not preached about it as much as I ought to have done. O sinner, when that dreadful wrath shall have fully come, whither can you flee for succor and where can you hide?

While I was in New York many years ago, I had a dream which made a strong impression on my mind. I never give heed at all to dreams unless they serve to impress great truths; then, they are of real use. In this dream, I heard awful thunders in one direction. Going to look out upon the face of the sky in that quarter, I was startled to find that the awful cloud had wholly overspread the sky and the thunders rolled from every quarter—the whole heavens seeming to be a burning mass of flame. Turning my eye downward to the earth, I saw the public square and all the streets, far as the eye could reach, crowded full of men and women, on their knees, wailing in utter agony and terror. I rushed out and pressed my way among them to offer Christ to their agonized souls. Look here, said I, how can you know but you may find mercy in Jesus, even now! Possibly, it may yet be in time! But to my amazement and grief, not one would hear me! Alas! Despair was upon them! Her iron grasp had seized upon their souls and there was no escape. Then I saw, as I had never seen before, why sinners cannot and will not repent in the world of despair.

I sometimes hear people sneer at the idea of "the wrath of the Lamb." May God help them see their madness! If the Lamb of God who dies for sinners becomes the Lion of His wrath, so much the more awful must His vengeance be! Sinner, will you still go on resisting all the claims of God and holding back His truth, so that it shall never save your soul? Having done this all your life thus far, will you do it yet again? How awful! Before God, I charge you today with the great crime of all crimes—holding back the truth of God from its legitimate influence on your soul. Do you ask what truth? This: Salvation possible today—offered freely to your dying soul. God calling for the free consecration of your heart, and you refusing. God saying, "Come," and your soul responding, "No!" No salvation, no yielding of your heart to Jesus! When Jesus lifts up His melting voice saying, "Come unto me for life," you answer, "No! You shall not have my heart. You shall not have my soul!" This is your ground. All the day long, this is your position: "I will not give God my heart. I will not have salvation at such a price." O, how unutterably horrible!*

---

* Charles G. Finney, "The Oberlin Evangelist," November 10, 1858. For Review: Answer the Study Questions on page 173, Cowles page 185.

3

Holding the Truth in Unrighteousness

1861

For the wrath of God is revealed from heaven against all ungodliness and unrighteousness of men, who hold the truth in unrighteousness; Because that which may be known of God is manifest in them; for God hath showed it unto them.—Romans 1:18-19—KJV

The wrath of God is being revealed from heaven against all the godlessness and wickedness of men who suppress the truth by their wickedness, since what may be known about God is plain to them, because God has made it plain to them.—Romans 1:18-19—NIV

The original word "ungodliness" means, primarily, to neglect God. It is the omission of duty to God; withholding worship from God, withholding love, confidence, and obedience from God. It is the withholding from God that which is due God.

The original word "unrighteousness" properly means, neglect of duty to others, as ungodliness implies neglect of duty to God. It is an omission

35

of duty, a withholding from others what is due them.

Unrighteousness, as the term is evidently used here in distinction from ungodliness, means the withholding of that equal love to others which is their due—that regard for their interests, feelings, character, and whatever is to them a good. Withholding this from others is unrighteousness, as withholding it from God is ungodliness. Unrighteousness, in the broader sense, consists in withholding, either from God or others, whatever is their due from us. But, as the terms ungodliness and unrighteousness are both used here, we are undoubtedly to understand unrighteousness here as having reference particularly to the omission of duty to others. Therefore, everything is unrighteousness which is short of doing our whole duty to others. Everything is ungodliness which is short of doing our whole duty to God.

What does it mean to "hold the truth in unrighteousness"?

The word rendered "hold" in this case means "to restrain," to hold down, to hold back. To hold the truth in unrighteousness is for selfish reasons to refuse to obey the truth. When duty is once known or seen, indifference is impossible. Truth is the natural stimulus of the mind, and especially truth that reveals moral obligation. When moral obligation is perceived, the mind cannot remain inactive. The perception of moral obligation forces the mind into a state of activity. The *Freedom of the Will* does not imply that in such circumstances the mind can remain inactive altogether. The *Freedom of the Will* implies that in every case of perceived moral obligation we have power to act one way or the other, to comply or refuse compliance with moral obligation. When, therefore, moral obligation is perceived, passivity becomes impossible. The mind must act. The mind must either comply with the obligation or refuse to comply. This should always be remembered—indifference, or a state of non-activity, becomes impossible in the presence of perceived obligation. In such circumstances, truth must be embraced or rejected. Obligation must be accepted or rejected. Duty must be performed or neglected. If you "hold the truth in unrighteousness," you withhold your heart and your life from obeying even though you know the truth and know you ought to obey.

Holding the truth in unrighteousness is to persist in neglecting your duty when you see your obligation and are convinced of your obligation.

To hold the truth in unrighteousness is to refuse to perform duty when it is known. Neglect in these circumstances is real refusal. There cannot be neglect in the sense of no action at all. The mind must act in opposition, must gird itself and refuse, in order to neglect when obligation is known. To hold the truth in unrighteousness, then, is precisely this—when people perceive and admit their obligation to others they selfishly refuse to meet the obligation.

To hold the truth in unrighteousness is to unjustly neglect or refuse to perform our duty to God or man. Ungodliness, or withholding from God, is injustice or unrighteousness toward God. All who neglect to perform their duty either to God or others are guilty of holding the truth in unrighteousness in the sense of this text.

What are we to understand by "the wrath of God"?

The wrath of God is not a selfish anger such as selfish people exercise; but a benevolent, holy indignation, such in kind as a benevolent father or ruler might exercise toward injustice, selfishness, and madness in an undutiful child or subject. The term is a strong one. By "wrath," we mean something more than mere anger in a low degree. It implies an intense indignation.

Against whom is this wrath of God revealed from heaven?

The wrath of God is revealed against all persons who do not act upon and up to their conviction in respect to their duty either to God or man. It is a very common thing to find persons admitting that such and such things they ought to do, and there they stop. They seem to make a virtue of admitting their obligation in words, while they deny it in action. You press them with their obligation, and they will say, "O yes, I know that I ought"—but what then? There they stop and do not lift a finger to perform their duty. Now, against all such persons whether they profess Christianity or not, the wrath of God is revealed from heaven.

The wrath of God is revealed from heaven against all who allow themselves shortcomings. I say allow themselves shortcomings in respect either to God or man. It is not an uncommon thing for persons, in looking back, to accuse themselves of shortcomings, when after all they are not aware of having deliberately and knowingly, at the time, fallen short of their duty. But observe, I say that the wrath of God is revealed against all *who allow themselves* shortcomings—who are aware of their duty and really indulge themselves in neglect and shortcomings. As if a man owed a debt to a neighbor, and then knowingly and deliberately neglected to pay him. When an individual admits his obligation to love, to confide in, to worship and obey God, and indulges himself in disobedience, or allows himself to neglect to perform his duty to God; against all such, the wrath of God is revealed from heaven.

The wrath of God is revealed from heaven against all who stop short of living up to their privileges, as well as their duty. It is really your duty to live up to your privileges. A man cannot allow himself to live below his privileges, without at the same time allowing himself to live below his duties. It is certainly a man's duty to avail himself of all the means within his reach of promoting his own holiness and usefulness in the highest degree; and to stop short of this, for selfish reasons, is a great crime against God. Therefore the wrath of God is revealed against all who do this.

The wrath of God is revealed from heaven against all who *rest and stop short* of full sanctification, full obedience to God, as they understand their duty. I say, stop short; by which I mean that they knowingly quiet themselves in this state of shortcoming. A great many who profess Christianity seem to have very little anxiety about not being entirely sanctified and fully obeying God. If they can believe themselves safe, they seem very well satisfied; although they know they are indulging in more or less sin from day to day. It is not with them a matter of intense struggle and effort to render to God full obedience. It is enough for them that they think themselves justified; the question of sanctification they are very willing to postpone. They say they do not believe in sanctification in this life. They seem to throw up the reins and live on loosely, talk about continually sinning and repenting; while it is evident enough that they do not care to render to God a full and continued obedience. They care but little for sin if they can be forgiven. They care but little about sanctification, if they can ensure justification. Now it is perfectly plain that the wrath of God is revealed from heaven against all such persons who are living on in known and allowed shortcomings in regard to sanctification—sinning and sinning and caring little about it—being anxious only to know that they are safe. The fact is, such persons are not safe. You should understand this at once: you are as far as possible from being safe. You are under the wrath of God which is revealed from heaven against you. You are knowingly and carelessly withholding from God what is due Him. You are allowing yourself in sin, caring more for your justification than for your sanctification. Be not deceived, for God is not mocked. You cannot make God believe that you are a sincere Christian, while you are so careless about sanctification. What is sanctification but full obedience to God? Can you make God believe that you are a sincere Christian, while you are careless about rendering to Him in all things a full obedience?

The wrath of God is revealed from heaven against all whose religion is of the negative rather than of the positive kind. The law of God is positive. It requires supreme love to God and equal love to others. It requires action toward God and man, intense action, energetic devotion to God and man. Now there are many who seem to suppose that religion is "doing nothing bad," as they say. They run hither and thither, and indulge themselves, and live in most things like the world around them. Their way of spending their time, of spending their money, of using their influence, is such that you ask, "Why do they do this, and why they do that?" "Why!" they reply, "What harm is there in it?" With them, the question is, "What harm is there in this or that course of life?" Not, "What good will this do?" Not, "How far will it glorify God?" If they live without committing flagrant sins, they think they do well. It does not seem so much as to enter into their designs to do all they can for the promotion of God's glory, but only to avoid doing such things as will be an open disgrace to Christianity. Their religion is a mere negation, if you can call it "religion;" which, indeed it cannot properly be, for all true religion is love, confidence, worship, obedience to the true God. Let all such, then, who are satisfying themselves with this negative form of what they call religion, remember that the wrath of God is revealed from heaven against them.

There are some whose history seems to be one of omission. They are continually neglecting many forms of duty. They know it. Perhaps some of you here are admitting from day to day that this, and that, and the other thing is your duty; and yet you never address yourselves seriously to the performance of it.

Some of you are perhaps neglecting secret prayer—are neglecting your Bible—are neglecting to pay your debts—are neglecting in the outward life a great multitude of things. In regard to God and man, and in your inward state, you cannot but know that you are really neglecting to render to God all the love and confidence that are His due, and that you are neglecting to love your neighbor as yourself. Your history is one of omission. You seem to overlook the fact that omission is the very thing against which this text is arrayed. Ungodliness and unrighteousness are omissions of duty to God and man.

You seem also to forget that omission is a real withholding, a real refusal. It is not a state of inaction, but of contrary action—a girding yourself to resist the claims of God and the claims of duty. Your omission is not a mere passive state, but a state of selfish activity; the omitting to perform your duty to God and man for the sake of gratifying yourself. Now can you not, some of you, right here, accuse yourself of living a life of omission? Is not this the history of your religion? Are you not acknowledging from day to day in your conscience that you owe this, and that, and the other duty to God and man; while you are neglecting to perform these duties? Now remember, if this is so, the wrath of God is revealed from heaven against you. If you are neglecting any heart duty, or any outward duty—and if you allow yourselves in this neglect or continue to indulge in this omission, you are as far as possible from being safe. I pray you, lay this to heart.

The wrath of God is revealed from heaven against all sinners who neglect repentance and faith; in other words, who neglect to become Christians.

The wrath of God is revealed from heaven against all sinners who neglect God, who neglect prayer, and who neglect to perform all the duties enjoined upon every son and daughter of Adam.

The wrath of God is revealed from heaven against all procrastinators, whether in or out of the church. By procrastinators, I mean those who have it in their mind at some future time to perform their duty; and who for some reason put it off for the present. This is the great sin of many persons. They know their duty—they know that now is the accepted time and now is the day of salvation. But for unrighteous reasons they continue to procrastinate, to put God off.

The wrath of God is revealed from heaven against all sinners who neglect to do and be what God requires Christians to do and be. All to whom the gospel is preached are bound to be Christians immediately. A great many sinners are constantly watching Christians and accusing them, but they seem not to understand that God requires of them what He requires of Christians. In condemning Christians, they only condemn themselves. In pointing out the shortcomings of Christians, they only point out their own. Now sinners, what you suppose God requires of Christians, you are bound to perform yourselves. You seem to know what the Christian's duty is; you continue to judge the Christian, and therefore you show that you know what he ought to do and what he ought to be. But, if you neglect to do and to be what you require of a Christian, then you fall short of your known duty, and the wrath of God is revealed from heaven against you for not doing what you expect of Christians.

The wrath of God is revealed from heaven against all who know better than they habitually do. Now all sinners are in this state. This is what constitutes them sinners. They know better than they do. They know their duty, but they do it not. This is that for which the wrath of God is revealed against them.

Impenitent sinners are very apt to think of their sins only as commissions of something in the outward life; but they seldom think much of their neglects of duty to God or others. However, it should be understood that all sin resolves itself into either neglect or refusal to render to God and others their due. Indeed, there are many, both those professing to be Christians and those not professing to be Christians, who live habitually in opposition to their convictions of duty. Now let it be understood that this is the very essence of sin. Against all such persons the wrath of God is revealed from heaven. In making righteous judgments, God must reveal

3

Romans 1:18-19

His indignation and displeasure toward all impenitent sinners.

Why does God reveal His wrath against these sins?

Neglect of duty implies knowledge of duty. You cannot say a person neglects a duty of which he has no knowledge. Neglect of duty implies ability to perform it. A person cannot be truly said to neglect that which he has no power to perform. Neglect of duty implies a refusal to do duty. Indeed, it involves it. A state of passivity in the presence of perceived obligation is impossible. Neglect of duty must involve deliberate and persistent disobedience to God.

Neglect of known duty to God or others involves a rejection of God's authority as not a sufficient reason for action. It is virtually saying, "What if God does require me to do such and such a thing? That is no good reason why I should do it. Who is God that I should obey Him, or what profit should I have if I should pray to Him?" Neglect of known duty involves a most insolent and contemptuous rejection of God's command as being a sufficient reason for action in that direction.

Holding the truth in unrighteousness involves a deliberate rejection of moral obligation as constituting an influential reason for action. Observe, in this case, the sinner knows his duty, he admits the obligation in words, but he rejects it in practice. What is this but saying, "What do I care for moral obligation? To be sure, I admit that there is a moral obligation; but what do I care? Do you suppose that I will be influenced by moral obligation? If you do, you do not know me. I hope you do not think that I am so weak as to yield to a mere moral obligation—to a mere command of God—to a mere sense of duty. Not I."

Holding the truth in unrighteousness involves a contempt for the idea of duty as being of no real practical account. "Duty!" says the sinner, "do you think I care for duty? What! My duty to God, and my duty to my neighbor? Do not talk to me of duty! What do I care for duty?" This holding the truth in unrighteousness is a real contempt for duty. It is virtually saying, "You never need expect me to be influenced by that consideration. You never need to tell me of my duty, for I care not for it. I will pursue my inclination, duty in any wise to the contrary notwithstanding.

Why do you come to me whining about the idea of duty, and tell me it is my duty to do thus, and thus, and thus? Away with your cant! I will have nothing to do with duty."

Holding the truth in unrighteousness involves a real ruling down of all moral considerations—the consideration of duty to God, the consideration of God's authority, the consideration of God's rights, of human rights, and of all rights. It is just ruling them down; putting your foot upon them; trampling them under your feet; and saying, "These considerations shall never influence me!"

This course of conduct in holding the truth in unrighteousness, in holding the mind back from obedience, is of course decisive of the moral attitude. It is taking a deliberate stand against God. It is taking a deliberate open stand before all His subjects, and pouring contempt upon His authority, upon His moral government, and upon all the moral considerations with which He attempts to enforce obedience. It is then taking the attitude of an open rebel, an open enemy, a persistent opponent of God.

Holding the truth in unrighteousness is decisive of moral character. It is a state of total depravity, of total dishonesty with regard to God and others. While the debt is admitted "in words," and the obligation to God and others "in words" is admitted, yet practically it is a denial of the obligation. The sinner virtually says, "I know I ought to obey God, but I will not. I know I ought to love my neighbor as myself, but I will not. I know I am indebted to God, but I will not pay him. I know I am indebted to others, but I do not care. I will not pay them what I owe them." This, then, is making an open issue with God before the entire universe. It is a deliberate, known, practical, persistent rejection of God's authority. It is setting the worst possible example before God's subjects.

Suppose a subject of any government to stand forth in the presence of all the subjects, and deliberately refuse to obey the laws; not merely refuse to obey some one law, but refuse to obey the laws in general and universally. Suppose the subject admitted the obligation. Suppose he admitted the wisdom and justice, and equity, and necessity of the laws, but for unrighteous reasons refused to obey them— to take a course directly opposed to them; to persist in that course, and to hold fast his persistent resistance to the authority of the government—should not the wrath of

3

Romans 1:18-19

the government be revealed against such a character as that? In His righteous indignation, God should reveal His wrath against such a person.

Holding the truth in unrighteousness is the deliberate refusal to pay an acknowledged debt to God. Suppose someone is indebted to you. You greatly need your money, and you go to him and demand it. He acknowledges the debt in terms, and you request him to pay it. He has the money; but he prefers to use it in some other way, to promote his own interest. You urge his obligation upon him. You tell him he ought to pay it, and he laughs you in the face, and says, "What do I care for that? Do you suppose I will be influenced by such a consideration as that? Oughtness! Shall oughtness influence me? Never!" But you remind him of the authority of God, and of His command to pay his debts. He laughs again, and says. "And who is God? And what do I care for God's commandments? Do you suppose I am to be influenced by such a consideration as that? Never!" Now you would feel, in such a case as this, that such a deliberate refusal, and such a contempt of obligation, was a dreadful sin against you.

See that negligent person who professes to be a Christian, see that impenitent sinner, deliberately refusing to pay an acknowledged debt to God; virtually saying to God, "What do I care for your authority? What do I care for my obligations to You? I will not be influenced by an obligation to pay my debts either to God or man." Suppose a child should take such a stand as this toward his parents. What if your child deliberately, habitually, and universally neglected obedience—refused, omitted, all obedience—what would you say of such a child? Should not the parents be angry? Should not they reveal their indignation against that child?

What would you say of your debtor, in case he should treat you in such a way? Would you not feel yourself called upon to put him in a way to pay you, if he deliberately despised all obligation for selfish reasons and deliberately refused to pay an acknowledged debt? Suppose in this case you should go and sue him, and bring him before a court, and he should say, "Why, you appear to be displeased, you appear to feel indignant that I do not pay you." Would you not reply, "I have reason to be indignant. You are a scoundrel. You are a dishonest man. You despise all moral obligation. I will see what I can do by enforcing legal obligation. You treat all moral obligation with contempt; and what is left to me but to compel you to pay your debt?"

So in the case of holding the truth in unrighteousness. Obligation to God is treated with contempt. God himself is treated with contempt. His authority is treated as a mere trifle. His feelings are outraged and despised. Is it not appropriate for God to be "angry with the wicked every day?" God should have a benevolent indignation toward those who thus despise their obligation. Is it not appropriate in Him to express or reveal this indignation, this wrath from heaven against such conduct as this? What would you think of a human ruler who should let such conduct pass without manifesting the least displeasure at it? Or a parent who should let such conduct pass without manifesting any displeasure at it. The fact is, God has infinitely good reasons for being highly displeased. His wrath must be enkindled against all ungodliness and unrighteousness of men, who hold the truth in unrighteousness.

Now, what will be said of Him if He does not manifest this wrath? What will His subjects think of Him? Can they maintain their confidence in Him? Will He not forfeit their confidence? Will He not inevitably lose the confidence of all His faithful subjects, if He neglects to manifest or reveal His wrath against all ungodliness and unrighteousness of men, who hold the truth in unrighteousness?

REMARKS

From this standpoint, we can see the awful delusions of mere moralists. There are many who totally neglect God, and are, therefore, in the sense of this text, emphatically ungodly. They withhold from God the love, confidence, obedience, and worship which is His due, and still imagine that they are doing nothing very wrong. You speak of their danger of being lost—they are ready to say, "Why, what have I done that is bad? Whom have I wronged?" Now the answer is plain, in the light of this text. You have wronged God. You have never performed your duty to Him in any sense or degree.

What if you should refuse to pay your debts to others? Suppose you were indebted to many and never paid them the first cent—habitually

45

and universally neglected to meet their just demands; and then you should set up for a moral man—should ask, "What evil have I done?" Suppose your creditors should often demand their pay, and you should as often acknowledge in words that the debts were just, and you ought to pay them. But still, you neglect and refuse to pay them, and never pay them at all. And then, suppose they should complain of you, and you should say, "Why, what have I done?" Would not this be ridiculous?

But this is the manner in which you treat God. You make little or no account of your neglect to pay what you owe to God. You would feel intensely if anybody owed you, and if others should treat their obligation to you as you treat your obligation to God. Just think! You are perfectly ungodly, and yet laying the flattering unction to your soul that you have done nothing very bad. But you have neglected your whole duty to others as well as to God. The law of God and the law of your own conscience requires you to love your neighbor as yourself; to regard and treat his interests as your own; to be careful of his reputation as of your own, of his feelings as of your own, of his interests as of your own. Now, have you done this? You satisfy yourself by saying you have not wronged him. Wronged him! Have you not withheld from him that which is his due? Have you not refused to love him? Refused to be interested in his welfare? Have you cared for his soul? Have you done anything to save him?

Suppose you had seen him asleep in his house with the house on fire, and you had allowed it to burn down and consume him, and had given him no warning; and then you should say, "Wherein have I wronged him?"

The fact is, you have wronged both God and others. You have withheld from God and others their due. You have no more right to claim to be a moral person than Satan has a claim to be a moral angel. A mere moralist, an unconverted person, a person who neglects his duty to God and others, as all unconverted sinners do, is void of all moral honesty.

Why, how ridiculous for you to pretend to be morally honest, when you refuse, universally, to pay your debts. You do not hesitate to treat the claims of God, which you admit to be just, with utter contempt in your practice. You withhold from Him all that is really valuable to Him. For, if you do not love Him, if you do not regard His interests, your outward life, if it appears to be an honest and moral life, is a mere hypocrisy. Your kind treatment of others is not, and cannot be, because you love them. For, if you are a mere moralist, an unconverted person, you do not love your neighbor as yourself. You must, therefore, have some other reason than love to your neighbor for treating him kindly. It must be some other reason than real honesty of heart and uprightness before God and others that gives you any appearance of honesty.

Suppose a person owed you and was under every possible obligation to you and yet should despise the whole, and never perform his duty, or pay you a debt, or discharge any obligation. Could you believe him an honest man? No, you could not believe that he had one particle of moral honesty in him.

Suppose you should see a son who treated his own parents as you treat God. Would you believe that son an honest man, however much he might boast of honesty? Would you not be convinced irresistibly that any man that could treat honorable and upright parents with the contempt with which you treat God could not be an honest man? Would you not regard him as void of all moral honesty? Would you not say irresistibly, a man that can do that has no honesty in his soul? I beseech you to lay aside the claim of honesty and morality, and take home to yourself the charge that you are a totally dishonest and base person, one who has no real claim to be regarded as anything other than a wicked, unprincipled, selfish being.

The same must be said of many who claim to be Christians. What an awful delusion they are under! Supposing themselves to have been converted, they live on in habitual and known transgression. Many things which they acknowledge to be their duty, they never pretend to perform. They allow themselves all the time to live in the neglect of what everybody knows and they themselves acknowledge to be their duty; and yet they think they are justified. They think they are penitent. But what idea can they have of repentance? Is not repentance the renunciation of sin? But what is sin but withholding from God and others their due? Here then is a professing Christian who habitually withholds from God and others their due, living on in known omissions; and confessing his omission, and will continue to confess them without end, and never address himself to the performance of these duties. Now what a delusion is this!

Why, on the very face of it, it is hypocrisy and a fatal delusion.

This text does not agree with the doctrine of moral inability, about which we hear so much. There are many who are continually ready to acknowledge their shortcomings, and acknowledge in words their crime. But they plead their inability to obey. Inability! And does this text teach or imply any such doctrine as that? Why, this text assumes the very opposite of the doctrine of moral inability. It takes the ground that people, so far from being unable to obey the commands of God, are positively resisting them. And this is in fact true!

I have already said that truth, and especially the truth of moral obligation, is the natural stimulus of the mind. Truth wakes it up, and compels the mind to act in one way or the other. Moral obligation will at once enlist and engage the energies of the soul. Unless a person actively and positively suppresses the truth, unless he holds back and restrains the truth in unrighteousness, his mind will surely obey it. Here then, instead of being unable to obey, the individual is obliged to gird himself to resist in order to prevent obedience. Truth is a mighty impulse to draw him into conformity with itself; but, for selfish reasons, he girds himself and holds it back, restrains it in unrighteousness. This then, is your moral inability, sinner and professing Christian. Truth, if you did not restrain it, would at once quicken you into activity and into obedience, but you harden your heart and you stiffen your neck, and you resist the claims of truth and of God. This is plainly the doctrine of this text, as it is of the Bible universally when properly understood.

People feel that neglect is sin, when they themselves are the object of neglect. Parents feel that the neglect of their children is sin. Husbands and wives feel that the neglect of the other party is sin. Those in business feel that it is sin in their debtors if they neglect to pay them, especially where this neglect is owing, not to financial inability, but to selfishness, or carelessness of the rights of others. Selfish people are loud in their complaints of others who neglect to pay their debts to them; but it would surely be more consistent for them to cease complaining of anybody's neglecting them, while they are neglecting to pay their debt to God. You who complain that others neglect to pay their debts to you, do you neglect to pay your debts to God?

How little stress is laid upon the neglect of duty as being a sin. Always remember that the law of God is positive. God is never satisfied with a someone doing nothing. God requires people to act, and that with all their heart, and soul, and mind, and strength. When God is totally neglected, when people are ungodly and unrighteous, neglecting their duty to God and others, how strange it is that this neglect should be so little regarded as a great and abominable sin against God, and as indeed the essence of all sin.

Church discipline is often a great obstacle on this account. Some are allowed to live in fellowship with the churches and neglect their duty habitually and notoriously. Some are allowed to neglect their duties to the church and their duty to God, and live cold and formal lives, and do not hesitate in words to confess it, while they do not reform. How strange it is that some are allowed to remain in the church as accepted members, who so neglect their duty both to God and others.

Sinners are misled by the church in this respect. Children in Christian families see that their parents are living in constant neglect of duty. If they attend meetings, they hear Christians confessing that they are constantly neglecting duty, and they know very well that they expect to continue to neglect their duty. Yet very little stress is laid upon this by the church or by the ministry. Now this fatally misleads many sinners. They come to think but very little of the omission of duty. The example of the church on this subject is the greatest obstacle to understanding and belief to them. They hear their parents say that they neglect God, and they neglect duty. Very well how little, then, do they think of neglecting their duty!

It has come to this, that the example of the Church in this respect has completely stumbled the world; so that sinners are living for scores of years in the neglect of all their duty to God, and yet do not consider themselves as very bad sinners. They say they have done nothing very bad. Now how did they come to this idea? The fact is, they have learned it from the church. They have been in the habit of hearing church members speak of the omission and neglect of duty as an almost natural thing.

Theologically orthodox neglectors of duty are the greatest sinners in the world. I have said that neglect of duty implies a knowledge of duty. Now the more orthodox in sentiment people are, and the more enlightened people are, the greater, surely, is their obligation. Those, therefore, who are truly orthodox in sentiment, but heterodox in practice, living in the neglect of their known duty, are the greatest sinners in the world. From this standpoint, we can also see the actual difference between real saints and sinners. I have just spoken of professing Christians who live in the habitual neglect of duty, and of the church so largely composed of mere nominal professing Christians, as being an obstacle to belief and understanding to the world. Remember, then, that I am now about to speak, not of nominal "Christians," of negligent souls, but of real saints and sinners. I also wish to be understood as meaning by enemies all who live in the habitual neglect of known duty. Saints are converted persons; sinners are unconverted. Saints are penitent souls; sinners are impenitent. Saints are obedient; sinners are disobedient. Saints are God's friends; sinners are God's enemies. Both saints and sinners know their duty; saints do their duty; but sinners omit theirs.

With the true saint, knowing God's will is reason enough. The true saint wants no further reason to influence his conduct. Such is God's will; with the true saint this is enough. This state of mind constitutes him a saint. He has given up his spirit of disobedience. He has ceased to hold truth in unrighteousness. He has yielded his mind to the influence of truth. He has accepted God's will, and he has laid aside his rebellion and become an obedient subject of Christ. Now mark this! He wants no better or higher reason for any course of conduct than to know that such is the will of Christ.

With the sinner, the opposite is true. He knows his duty, but this is no influential reason with him at all. He has not accepted the will of God as his rule of life. He affirms it to be his duty to do so, but he does not do it. This constitutes him an impenitent sinner. The revealed will of God is no sufficient reason at all to induce obedience with him. He knows his duty, perhaps as well as the saint does, but he does not do it. He holds the truth in unrighteousness.

With the true saint, the omission of any duty is a dreadful thing. What! To disobey a command of God! To know that God requires of him a certain course of action, and for him to refuse! Why, it is a dreadful thing! A thing not to be thought of! But, with the impenitent sinner, the omission of duty is a mere trifle, a thing scarcely worth considering. He goes forward omitting all his duty, and all with as little consideration, or fear, or regret, as he would have in view of any trifle that you can name.

This text is more frequently suggested by facts around us than almost any other in the Bible. It is so very common to find people neglecting what they know and even confess to be their duty, and it is utterly amazing when we consider that so many of these confessors claim to be Christians. They confess themselves to be in the habitual neglect of some duties, and perhaps of many, and yet they profess they are the children of God. They profess to be converted, to be God's saints, His holy ones. Now, who can live in such surroundings without being constantly reminded of this text: "The wrath of God is revealed from heaven against all ungodliness and unrighteousness of men, who hold the truth in unrighteousness." The announcement of this text ought to shock such persons like a thunder bolt. See these dreamers! This multitude of souls that are crying, "Peace, Peace," when there is no peace! Neglecting their duty to God and others! Hark! Hear the thunder of this text, and let your nerves tremble!

Ministers have reason to tremble for their hearers. How perfectly common it is for ministers to preach and hold out the claims of God, while their people will confess that it is truth, and that so they ought to do, but do they do it? Let such a minister watch his people. He holds out to them on the Sabbath the claims of God, and they go away, perhaps eulogizing the preaching; at any rate they confess that they have been instructed in regard to their duty—but does he find them the next day, and every subsequent day, addressing themselves to their duty? Does he expect them to do it? Does he even expect his own church to do it? I should like to ask ministers, how many members of their church do they have reason to believe, from acquaintance with them, will do their duty as soon as they are instructed in regard to it. And I should like to ask them if it is not true that in a great multitude of instances, they have no expectation at all that the members of their church will wake up and be influenced by the truth, and will do what they know to be their duty. After preaching on the Sabbath and holding out to the church the claims of God, would they not be surprised on Monday to see the church all astir, and full of energy and vigor in carrying out their instructions on the Sabbath? How common it is for ministers to hold out the claims of God, to pour the truth upon their hearers; and then to see, right before their faces, that they hold the truth in unrighteousness. They know and acknowledge their duty, but they do not do it.

Let us reflect that it is the wrath of God that is revealed from heaven against all ungodliness and unrighteousness of those who hold the truth in unrighteousness. It is the wrath of God, and therefore it cannot be resisted. It is the wrath of God, and therefore it cannot be endured. "Can your heart endure, can your hand be strong in the day that I shall deal with you, says the Lord? What then will you do in the day when I shall punish you?" Sinner and negligent professing "Christian," have you really considered what it is to have the wrath of an Omnipresent and Almighty Being revealed from heaven against you? Revealed from heaven! See, the holy mount is covered with dark clouds, the batteries are charged, the match is lighted, and the Almighty is there!

Are you not afraid to pursue your course of neglect of duty, holding truth in unrighteousness? In just such a time as you think not, and when you are crying peace and safety, these batteries of Omnipotence will open upon you—the discharge will wither you in a moment—and you will sink down, down, down in the blackness of darkness forever!

What then shall you do? I answer, immediately discard this spirit of delay—lay hold upon eternal life—let your heart go to Christ—no longer hold the truth in unrighteousness. Arise, and what you do, do quickly. Lay hold upon eternal life; for "now is the accepted time, behold, now is the day of salvation" (2 Corinthians 6:2—KJV).*

---

* Charles G. Finney, "The Oberlin Evangelist," August 14 and August 28, 1861, *Principles of Liberty*, 23–36. For Review: Answer the Study Questions on page 174, Cowles page 185.

4

On The Atonement
1856

The LORD is well pleased for his righteousness' sake; he will magnify the law, and make it honourable.—Isaiah 42:21—KJV

It pleased the LORD for the sake of his righteousness to make his law great and glorious.—Isaiah 42:21—NIV

Whom God hath set forth to be a propitiation through faith in his blood, to declare his righteousness for the remission of sins that are past, through the forbearance of God; To declare, I say, at this time his righteousness: that he might be just, and the justifier of him which believeth in Jesus.—Romans 3:25-26—KJV

God presented him as a sacrifice of atonement, through faith in his blood. He did this to demonstrate his justice, because in his forbearance he had left the sins committed beforehand unpunished—he did it to demonstrate his justice at the present time, so as to be just and the one who justifies those who have faith in Jesus.—Romans 3:25-26—NIV

But God commendeth his love toward us, in that, while we were yet sinners, Christ died for us. —Romans 5:8—KJV

But God demonstrates his own love for us in this: While we were still sinners, Christ died for us. —Romans 5:8—NIV

For I delivered unto you first of all that which I also received, how that Christ died for our sins according to the scriptures. —1 Corinthians 15:3—KJV

For what I received I passed on to you as of first importance: that Christ died for our sins according to the Scriptures. —1 Corinthians 15:3—NIV

For he hath made him to be sin for us, who knew no sin; that we might be made the righteousness of God in him. —2 Corinthians 5:21—KJV

God made him who had no sin to be sin for us, so that in him we might become the righteousness of God. —2 Corinthians 5:21—NIV

With unusual fullness, the Apostle Paul states the theological, and I might even say the philosophical, design of Christ's mission to our world; that is, to set forth before created beings God's righteousness in forgiving sins. Christ is presented as a propitiation, so God may be just in forgiving sins. God could not have been just to the universe unless Christ had been first set forth as a sacrifice.

When we seriously consider the irresistible convictions of our own minds concerning our relations to God and His government, we cannot but see that we are sinners. We are lost beyond hope on the score of law and justice. The fact that we are grievous sinners against God is an ultimate fact of human consciousness, testified to by our irresistible convictions, and we cannot deny the fact any more than we can deny that there is such a thing as wrong.

Since God is holy and good, He must not approve wrongdoing, and He will punish it. The penalty of His law is pronounced against wrongdoing. Under this penalty, we stand condemned, and we have no relief except through some adequate atonement, satisfactory to God and safe to the interests of His kingdom.

This far we may advance safely and be on solid ground by the simple light of nature. If there were no Bible, we might know this much with absolute certainty. So far, even infidels are compelled to reason thus.

We are under absolute and the most righteous condemnation. Is there any way of escape? If so, it must be revealed to us in the Bible; for from any other source it cannot come. The Bible does profess to reveal a method of escape. This is the great burden of its message.

Two great truths to always remember.

The Bible opens with a very brief allusion to the circumstances under which sin came into the world. Without being very detailed as to the manner in which sin entered the world, the Bible is exceedingly full, clear, and definite in showing the fact of sin in the human race. That God regards the human race as in sin and rebellion is made as plain as language can make it. It is worthy of notice that this fact and the connected fact of possible pardon are affirmed on the same authority—with the same sort of explicitness and clearness. These facts stand or fall together. Manifestly, God intended to impress on all minds these two great truths. First, people are ruined by their own sins. Second, people may be saved through Jesus Christ. To deny the former is to contradict both our own irresistible convictions and God's most explicit revealed testimony. To deny the latter, is to shut the door by our own free act and accord against all hope of our own salvation.

The fact of the atonement.

The philosophical explanation of the reasons and governmental bearings of the atonement must not be confused with the fact of the atonement. People may be saved by the fact of the atonement, if they simply believe it, while they may know nothing about the philosophical explanation. The apostles did not give much of an account regarding the explanation of the atonement, but they asserted the fact most earnestly, gave miracles as testimony to prove their authority from God, and so besought

4

Romans 3:25-26

people to believe the fact and be saved. The fact, then, may be savingly believed, and yet the explanation be unknown. This has been the case, no doubt, with scores of thousands.

Reasons for understanding the atonement.

Still, it is very useful to understand the reasons and governmental grounds of the atonement. It often serves to remove skepticism. It is very common for lawyers to reject the fact, until they come to see the reasons and governmental bearings of the atonement; this seen, they usually admit the fact. Many people need to see the governmental bearings of the atonement, or they will reject the fact of the atonement. The reason some people doubt the fact of the atonement is the explanations given have been unsatisfactory. The explanations have misrepresented God. No wonder people reject them, and with them, the fact of any atonement at all.

The atonement is a governmental expedient to sustain law without the execution of its penalty on the sinner. Of course, it must always be a difficult thing in any government to sustain the authority of the law, and the respect due to it, without the execution of the penalty. Yet God has accomplished it most perfectly.

A distinction between public and retributive justice.

Retributive justice visits on the head of the individual sinner a punishment corresponding to the nature of his offence. Public justice looks only toward the general good, and must do that which will secure the authority and influence of the law as well as inflicting the penalty would. Public justice may accept a substitute, provided it be equally effective to the support of law and the ensuring of obedience.

Public justice may be satisfied in one of two ways, either by the full execution of the penalty, or by some substitute, which will serve the ends or meet the goals of the government at least equally well. When, therefore, we ask, "What is necessary for the purpose of public justice to be achieved?" The answer involves the following.

To achieve public justice, the government does not need to execute literally the penalty of the law on the offender. To satisfy public justice, the punishment must not necessarily fall on the sinner. It would be no gain to the universe for Jesus Christ to suffer the full and exact penalty that is due to every lost sinner who would be saved by Him. The amount of suffering being the same in the one case as in the other, where is the gain? And yet, if the administration of justice is to be retributive, then it cannot fall on Christ, and must fall on the sinner himself. If not retributive, it certainly may be, as compared with that due the sinner, far different in kind and less in degree. It has sometimes been said that Christ suffered all in degree and the same in kind as all the saved must have suffered, but human reason revolts at this assumption, and certainly the scriptures do not affirm it.

Some claim that God must be appeased and have His feelings conciliated. This is an egregious mistake. This view utterly misrepresents God and misunderstands the atonement.

Satisfying public justice does not mean that an innocent being should suffer the penalty or punishment, in the proper sense of these terms. Punishment implies crime—Christ committed no crimes. Therefore, Jesus Christ was not punished.

Always understand that the divine law originates in God's benevolence, and has only benevolent goals. God revealed the Law only and solely to promote the greatest possible good by means of obedience. Now, God's Law can allow pardon, provided an expression can be given which will equally secure obedience—making an equal revelation of the lawgiver's firmness, integrity and love. The law being perfect, and being most essential to the good of His creatures, God must not set aside its penalty without some equivalent influence to induce obedience.

God designed the penalty for disobeying His law to be a testimony to His regard for the precept of His law, and of His purpose to uphold His law. An atonement, therefore, which should serve as a substitute for the infliction of this penalty, must be of such sort as to show God's great regard for both the precept and penalty of His law. It must be adapted to enforce obedience. Its moral power must be in this respect equal to that of the infliction of the penalty on the sinner. Consequently, we find that

4

Romans 3:25-26

in the atonement God has expressed His high regard for His law and for obedience to it.

The design of executing the penalty of the law was to make a strong impression of the majesty, excellence and utility of the law. Anything may serve as a substitute that will as thoroughly demonstrate the mischief and odiousness of sin, God's hatred of it, and His determination to carry out His law in all its demands. Especially, the proposed substitute must make a signal manifestation of God's love to sinners. The atonement, by the death of Jesus Christ, has most emphatically achieved God's purposes.

Every act of rebellion denounces the law. Hence, before God can pardon rebellion, He must make such a demonstration of His attitude toward sin as shall thrill the heart of the created universe and make every ear tingle. Especially, for the ends of the highest obedience, God needed to make such a demonstration as shall effectually secure the confidence and love of His subjects toward their Lawgiver—such as shall show that God is no tyrant, and that He seeks only the highest obedience and consequent happiness of His creatures. This done, God will be satisfied.

What can be done to teach these lessons?

What can be done to impress these lessons with great and everlasting emphasis on the universe? God must give His testimony in a way that is well understood. Obviously, the testimony to be given must come from God, for it is His view of the law, the penalty, and the substitute that needs to be revealed. Everyone must see that if God were to execute the penalty of disobedience on the sinner, this would show at once His view of the value of His law. Plainly, His view must be shown with equal force by any proposed substitute.

In the atonement, the precept of the law must be accepted and honored both by God the Father and by Jesus as the Mediator. Jesus Christ, as the representative of the human race, must honor the law by obeying it and by publicly endorsing it. Otherwise, Jesus would not manifest the required homage due the divine law in the atonement. Therefore, Jesus did honor the law of God by His life and words.

To make adequate provision for the exercise of mercy to the human race, it is plainly essential that, in the person of their Mediator, both the divine and the human should be united. God and man are both represented in the atonement. The divine Word represented the Godhead and the man Jesus represented the human race He came to redeem. What the Bible asserts is verified in the history of Jesus, for He said and did things which could not have been said and done unless He had been man, and equally could not have been said and done unless He were also God. On the one hand, Jesus Christ was too weak to carry His cross, because of the exhaustion of His human body. On the other hand, Christ was mighty to hush the storms and to raise the dead through the plenitude of divine power. Thus, Jesus Christ represented both God and man.

The law of God and the atonement required that Jesus Christ honor the law and fully obey it, and this He did. Standing for the sinner, He must, in an important sense, bear the curse of the law—not the literal penalty. But, He bore a vast amount of suffering, sufficient in view of His relations to God and the universe, to make the needed demonstration of God's displeasure against sin, and yet of His love for both the sinner and all His moral subjects. On the one hand, Jesus represented the human race; on the other, He represented God. This is a most divine philosophy.

The sacrifice of Jesus Christ made on Calvary is to be understood as God's offering to public justice. God himself giving up His Son to die, and God's Son pouring forth His life's blood in expiation for sin, and thus throwing open the folding gates of mercy to a sinning, lost race. The atonement must be regarded as manifesting God's love to sinners. This is God's ransom provided for them. Look at the state of the case. The supreme Lawgiver, and indeed the government of the universe, had been abused by rebellion; of course, there can be no pardon until this dishonor done to God and His law is thoroughly washed away. God did this by His free-will offering of His own Son for these great sins.

God provided the atonement for you, sinners, what do you think of it? What do you think of that appeal which Paul writes and God makes through him: "I beseech you, therefore, by the mercies of God, that ye present your bodies a living sacrifice, holy, acceptable to God, which is your reasonable service" (Romans 12:1—KJV)? Think of those mercies. Think how Christ poured out His life for you. Suppose He were to ap-

4

Romans 3:25-26

pear in the midst of you today, and hold up His hands dripping with blood, said, "I beseech you by the mercies shown you by God, that ye present your bodies a living sacrifice, holy, acceptable to God!" Would you not feel the force of His appeal that this is a "reasonable service?" Would not this love of Christ constrain and motivate you? What do you think of Christ's love for you manifested in the atonement? Jesus died for all, that those who live should not henceforth live unto themselves but unto Him that loved them and gave himself for them (see 2 Corinthians 5:14, 15). What do you say? Just as the uplifted ax would otherwise have fallen on your neck, He caught the blow on His own. You could have had no life if He had not died to save it; therefore, what will you do? Will you receive His offer of mercy or reject it? Yield to God the life that He has in mercy spared!

REMARKS

The governmental bearings of the atonement are perfectly apparent. The whole transaction tends powerfully to sustain God's law, and to reveal His love and mercy to sinners. The atonement shows that God is personally ready to forgive sinners, and He needs only to have such an arrangement made that He can do it safely as to His government. What could show His readiness to forgive more strikingly than the atonement? See how carefully God guards against the abuse of pardon! Always ready to pardon, yet ever watchful over the great interests of obedience and happiness, lest these interests be imperiled by the freeness and fullness of pardon!

Why should anyone think it incredible that God should devise such a plan of atonement? Is there anything in it that is unlike God, or inconsistent with His revealed character? I doubt whether any moral agent can understand this system and still think it incredible. Those who reject it as incredible must have failed to understand it.

Someone might ask, "Why did Christ die at all, if not for us?" He never sinned. He did not die on His own account as a sinner. He did not die as the infants of our human race do, with a moral nature yet undeveloped and who yet belong to a sinning race. The only account to be given of

Christ's death is that He died not for himself, but for us.

Someone else might ask, "Why did Jesus die so? See Him expiring between two thieves, and crushed down beneath a mountain weight of sorrow. Why was this? Other martyrs have died shouting; He died in anguish and grief, cast down and agonized beneath the apparent hidings of his Father's face. All nature seemed to sympathize with His sufferings. Notice: the sun clothed in darkness; the rocks were rent; the earth quaked beneath their feet; all nature is convulsed. Even a heathen philosopher exclaimed, "Surely the universe is coming to an end, or the Maker of the Universe is dying! Hark, that piercing cry, "My God, My God; why hast thou forsaken me?" (see Psalm 22:1 and Matthew 27:46—KJV).

Because Jesus died as a Savior for sinners, all is plain. He died for the government of God. He must suffer these things to make a just expression of God's abhorrence of sin. While He stands in the place of guilty sinners, God must frown on Him and hide His face. This reveals both the spirit of God's government and His own infinite wisdom.

Some have argued against the atonement, thinking that the atonement is likely to encourage sin. However, these persons neglect the very important distinction between the proper use of a thing and its abuse. No doubt, the best things in the universe may be abused, and by abuse be perverted to evil, and even more so, by how much the better they are in their legitimate use. The natural tendency of the atonement is good, and no one can rationally doubt this. The tendency of manifesting such love, meekness and self-sacrifice for sinners is to make the sinner trust and love God, to make him bow before the cross with a broken and contrite heart. Many do abuse the atonement. Unfortunately, too often, the best things, abused, become the worst. The abuse of the atonement is the very reason why God sends sinners to hell. The Bible says, "He that despised Moses' law died without mercy under two or three witnesses: Of how much sorer punishment, suppose ye, shall he be thought worthy, who hath trodden under foot the Son of God, and hath counted the blood of the covenant, wherewith he was sanctified, an unholy thing, and hath done despite unto the Spirit of grace?" (Hebrews 10:28, 29—KJV). Hence, if any sinner will abuse atoning blood, and trample down the holy law, and the very idea of returning to God in penitence and love, God will say of

4

Romans 3:25-26

him, "Of how much sorer punishment shall he be thought worthy" than he who despised Moses' law and fell beneath its vengeance?*

As a matter of fact, this manifestation of God in Christ does break the heart of sinners. It has subdued many hearts, and will thousands more. If they believe it and hold it as a reality, must it not subdue their heart to love God and express sorrow for sin? Do not you think so? Certainly if you saw it as it is, and felt the force of it in your heart, you would sob out on your very seat, break down and cry out: "Did Jesus love me so? Shall I love sin any more?" Ah, your heart would melt as thousands have been broken and melted in every age, when they have seen the love of Jesus as revealed on the cross. That beautiful hymn puts the case truthfully.

"I saw one hanging on a tree,
In agony and blood;
Who fixed his languid eyes on me,
As near the cross I stood."

But it was not his first look at Christ hanging on the cross that fully broke his heart. It was only when Christ said in a look to him,

"A second look he gave which said
I freely all forgive;
This blood is for thy ransom paid,
 I died that thou mayest live."**

that his whole heart broke, tears fell like rain, and he withheld no power of his being in the full consecration of his soul to this loving Savior. This is the genuine effect of the sinner's understanding the gospel and giving Jesus Christ full credit for His loving-kindness in dying for the lost. Faith thus breaks the stony heart. If this demonstration of God's love in Jesus Christ dying on the cross does not break your heart, nothing else will. If the sacrificial death and love of Christ do not inspire and motivate you to love and obey God, nothing else can.

If you will not look at the atonement of Christ, and will not set your mind upon His sacrificial love for sinners, the atonement will only work your ruin. To know this gospel only enough to reject and disown it can serve no other purpose except to make your guilt greater and your doom the more certain and fearful.

Jesus was made a sin-offering for us. How beautiful this was illustrated under the Mosaic system! The victim was brought out to be slain. The blood was carried in and sprinkled on the mercy-seat. This mercy-seat was no other than the sacred cover or lid of the ark which contained the tables of the law and other sacred memorials of God's ancient mercies. There they were in that deep recess—within which none might enter on pain of death except the High Priest, and he only once a year on the great day of atonement. On this eventful day, the sacred rites culminated to their highest solemnity. Two goats were brought forward upon which the high priest laid his hands and confessed publicly his own sins and the sins of all the people. Then one goat was driven far away into the wilderness, to signify how God removes our sins far as the east is from the west. The other goat was slain and its blood borne by the high priest into the most holy place, and sprinkled there upon the mercy-seat beneath the cherubim. Meanwhile, the vast congregation stood without, confessing their sins, and expecting remission only through the shedding of blood. It was as if the whole world had been standing around the base of Calvary, confessing their sins, while Jesus bore His cross to the summit, to hang thereon, and bleed and die for our sins. How fitting that, while Christ is dying, we should be confessing!

Some of you may think it a great thing to go on a foreign mission. However, Jesus Christ has led the way. He left Heaven on a foreign mission. He came down to this more than heathen world, and no one ever faced such self-denial. Yet He fearlessly marched up without the least hesitation to meet the consequences. Never did He shrink from disgrace, from humiliation, or torture or death. Can you shrink from following the footsteps of such a leader? Is anything too much for you to suffer, while you follow in the lead of such a Captain of your salvation? (see Hebrews 2:10)***

4

Romans 3:25-26

---

*Consider these verses in their context: "26 If we deliberately keep on sinning after we have received the knowledge of the truth, no sacrifice for sins is left, 27 but only a fearful expectation of judgment and of raging fire that will consume the enemies of God. 28 Anyone who rejected the law of Moses died without mercy on the testimony of two or three witnesses. 29 How much more severely do you think a man deserves to be punished who has trampled the Son of God under foot, who has treated as an unholy thing the blood of the covenant that sanctified him, and who has insulted the Spirit of grace? 30 For we know him who said, 'It is mine to avenge; I will repay,' and again, 'The Lord will judge his people.' 31 It is a dreadful thing to fall into the hands of the living God." (Hebrews 10:26-31—NIV)

** "Looking at the Cross" also known as "He Died for Me" by John Newton, the author of "Amazing Grace."

In evil long I took delight,
Unawed by shame or fear;
Till a new object struck my sight,
And stopped my wild career.

I saw one hanging on a tree,
In agonies and blood;
Who fixed his languid eyes on me,
As near his cross I stood.

Sure, never till my latest breath,
Can I forget that look;
It seemed to charge me with his death,
Though not a word he spoke.

My conscience felt, and owned the guilt,
And plunged me in despair;
I saw my sins his blood had spilt,
And helped to nail him there.

Alas! I knew not what I did,
But now my tears are vain;

Where shall my trembling soul be hid?
For I the LORD have slain.

A second look he gave, which said,
"I freely all forgive;
This blood is for thy ransom paid,
I die, that thou may'st live."

Thus, while his death my sin displays,
In all its blackest hue;
(Such is the mystery of grace)
It seals my pardon too.

With pleasing grief and mournful joy,
My spirit now is filled;
That I should such a life destroy,
Yet live by him I killed.

*** Charles G. Finney, "The Oberlin Evangelist," July 30, 1856, *Sermons on Gospel Themes*, 204–214, *Principles of Victory*, 38–45. For Review: Answer the Study Questions on page 175, Cowles page 191.

4

Romans 3:25-26

The Psalms on Righteousness

Lead me, O LORD, in your righteousness because of my enemies—make straight your way before me.—Psalm 5:8

I will give thanks to the LORD because of his righteousness and will sing praise to the name of the LORD Most High.—Psalm 7:17

He will judge the world in righteousness; he will govern the peoples with justice.—Psalm 9:8

And I—in righteousness I will see your face; when I awake, I will be satisfied with seeing your likeness.—Psalm 17:15

They will proclaim his righteousness to a people yet unborn—for he has done it.—Psalm 22:31

He restores my soul. He guides me in paths of righteousness for his name's sake.—Psalm 23:3

In you, O LORD, I have taken refuge; let me never be put to shame; deliver me in your righteousness.—Psalm 31:1

The LORD loves righteousness and justice; the earth is full of his unfailing love.—Psalm 33:5

My tongue will speak of your righteousness and of your praises all day long.—Psalm 35:28

Continue your love to those who know you, your righteousness to the upright in heart.—Psalm 36:10 (More on page 94)

5

Sanctification by Faith
1837

Do we then make void the law through faith? God forbid: yea, we establish the law.—Romans 3:31—KJV

Do we, then, nullify the law by this faith? Not at all! Rather, we uphold the law.—Romans 3:31—NIV

The Apostle Paul has been proving that everyone, Jews and Gentiles, are sinners. He has also been refuting the doctrine, so generally entertained by the Jews, that the Jews were a holy people and saved by their works. He showed that justification could never be by works, but only by faith. He then anticipated an objection similar to this, "Are we to understand you as teaching that the law of God is abrogated and set aside by this plan of justification?" "By no means," says the apostle, "we rather establish the law."

In discussing this, I shall show that the gospel method of justification by faith does not set aside or repeal the law. The gospel establishes the law by producing true obedience to it. The gospel is the only means that can produce true obedience.

The gospel method of justification does not set aside the law.

The greatest objection to the doctrine of "Justification by Faith" has always been that it is inconsistent with good morals, that it connives at sin and opens the floodgates of iniquity. Some have maintained that to teach people that they are not to depend on their own good behavior for salvation, but they are to place their faith in Jesus Christ to justify them, will make them disregard good morals and encourage them to live in sin. Others have maintained that the gospel does in fact release from obligation to obey the moral law, so that a more lax morality is permitted under the gospel than was allowed under the law.

The gospel method of justification does not set aside the moral law, and it cannot set aside the moral law, because the gospel everywhere enforces obedience to the law. The gospel lays down the same standard of holiness as the moral law. Jesus Christ adopted the very words of the moral law. "Jesus said unto him, 'Thou shalt love the Lord thy God with all thy heart, and with all thy soul, and with all thy mind. This is the first and great commandment. And the second is like unto it, Thou shalt love thy neighbor as thyself'" (Matt 22:37-39—KJV).

The conditions of the gospel are designed to sustain the moral law. The gospel requires repentance as a condition of salvation. What is repentance? Repentance is the renunciation of sin. People must repent of their breaches of the law of God and return to obedience of the moral law. This is tantamount to a requirement of obedience.

The gospel maintains that the law is right. If the gospel did not maintain the law to its full extent, it might be said that Jesus Christ is the minister or servant of sin. The gospel plan of salvation adds the sanctions of the gospel to the sanctions of the law to enforce obedience to the law.

The apostle wrote, "He that despised Moses' law died without mercy under two or three witnesses: Of how much sorer punishment , suppose ye, shall he be thought worthy, who hath trodden under foot the Son of God, and hath counted the blood of the covenant, wherewith he was sanctified, an unholy thing, and hath done despite unto the Spirit of grace?" (Hebrews 10:28-29—KJV). Thus, he adds the awful sanctions of the gospel to those of the law to enforce obedience to the precepts of the moral law.

Justification by faith produces true obedience.

The doctrine of "Justification by Faith" produces sanctification by producing the only true obedience to the law. When the mind understands the gospel plan of salvation and exercises faith in Jesus Christ, the gospel naturally produces sanctification in the believer. Sanctification is holiness, and holiness is nothing but obedience to the law, consisting in love to God and love to others.

In support of the proposition that justification by faith produces true obedience to the law of God, my first position is that sanctification never can be produced among selfish or wicked beings, by the law itself, separate from the considerations of the gospel, or the motives connected with justification by faith.

The motives of the law did not restrain sinners from committing sin. It is absurd to suppose the same motives can reclaim them from sin, when they have fallen under the power of selfishness, and when sin is confirmed by habit. The motives of the law lose a great part of their influence when a being is once fallen into sin. They even exert an opposite influence. The motives of the law, as viewed by a selfish mind, have a tendency to cause sin to abound. This is the experience of every sinner. When sinners see the spirituality of the law and do not see the motives of the gospel; then, pride increases in their hearts and confirms them in their rebellion. The case of the devil is an exhibition of what the law can do, with all its principles and sanctions, upon a wicked heart. The devil understands the law. The devil sees its reasonableness, and he experienced the blessedness of obedience prior to his rebellion against God. The devil knows full well that to return to obedience would restore his peace of mind. This he knows better than any sinner of our human race does. The devil knows God's law; yet, the moral law presents to his mind no motivation to reclaim him. On the contrary, God's law of love drives him a returnless

5

Romans 3:31

distance from obedience.

When you hold forth to the sinner obedience to the law of God as the condition of life, it immediately sets him upon making self-righteous efforts. In almost every instance, the first effort of the awakened sinner is to try to obey the law. He thinks he must first make himself better, in some way, before he may embrace the gospel. He has no idea of the simplicity of the gospel plan of salvation by faith, offering eternal life as a mere gratuitous gift. Alarm the sinner with the penalty of the law, and he naturally, and by the very laws of his mind, sets himself to do better, to amend his life, and in some self-righteous manner obtain eternal life, under the influence of slavish fear. The more the law presses him, the greater are his pharisaical efforts, while he still hopes that if he obeys he may be accepted. What else could you expect of him? He is purely selfish. Though he ought to submit at once to God, yet, as he does not understand the gospel terms of salvation, and his mind is of course first turned to the object of getting away from the danger of the penalty, he tries to get up to heaven some other way. I do not believe there is an instance in history of a person who has submitted to God until he has seen that salvation must be by faith, and that his own self-righteous strivings have no tendency to save him.

If you undertake to produce holiness by giving sinners legal motives, the very fear of failure has the effect of diverting their attention from the true objects of love, from God and Christ. The sinner is all the while compassing Mount Sinai, thinking of the Ten Commandments, and taking heed to his footsteps, to see how near he comes to obedience and how he can get into the spirit of heaven?

The penalty of the law has no tendency to produce love in the first instance. It may increase love in those who already have it, when they contemplate it as an exhibition of God's infinite holiness. The angels in heaven and good people on earth contemplate its propriety and fitness, and see in it the expression of the good will of God to His creatures. God's law appears amiable and lovely, and it increases their delight in God and their confidence toward Him. However, the reverse of this happens in the selfish person. The self-centered person sees the penalty hanging over his own head. He sees no way of escape. It is not in his mind to become enamored with the Being that holds the thunderbolt over his devoted head. From the nature of the human mind, the sinner will flee from God, not to Him. The inspired writers never dreamed that the moral law could sanctify sinners. They knew God revealed the penalty of the law to slay, not to make alive; to cut off the sinner's self-righteous hopes forever, and to compel them to flee to Christ for salvation.

Sinners, under the naked law and irrespective of the gospel, naturally and necessarily and of right, under such circumstances, view God as an irreconcilable enemy. Sinners are wholly selfish. Apart from the considerations of the gospel, they view God just as the devil views God. The law can present no motive to a selfish mind that will beget love. Can the influence of penalty for disobedience beget love for God?

Some have a strange view of reforming sinners! A strange plan of reformation is this: they think that to send them to hell will reform them! Let them go on in sin and rebellion to the end of their lives, and then punish them until they become holy. If this were possible, the devil would become holy! The devil has suffered long enough and has been in hell these thousands of years, yet he is no better than he was. The reason is this, there is no gospel in hell, and there is no Holy Spirit in hell to apply the truth; therefore, the penalty only confirms the sinner's rebellion.

The doctrine of "Justification by Faith" can relieve these difficulties. It can produce, and it has produced, real obedience to the precept of the law. Justification by faith does not set aside the law as a rule of duty, but only sets aside the penalty of the law. The preaching of justification by faith as a mere gratuity, bestowed on the simple act of faith, is the only way in which obedience to the law is ever established.

The gospel method is the only means to produce true obedience

Justification by faith is the only means of leading someone to true obedience, to loving God and others. Justification by faith relieves the mind from the pressure of those considerations that naturally tend to confirm selfishness. While the mind is looking only at the law, it only feels the influence of hope and fear, perpetuating purely selfish efforts. Justification by faith annihilates this spirit of bondage. The apostle wrote, "For ye have not received the spirit of bondage again to fear; but ye have received the Spirit of adoption, whereby we cry, 'Abba, Father'" (Romans 8:15—KJV). The gospel plan of salvation through justification by faith begets love and gratitude to God, and leads the soul to taste the sweets of holiness.

Justification by faith relieves the mind also from the necessity of making its own salvation its supreme object. Believers in the gospel plan of salvation find salvation, full and complete, including both sanctification and eternal life, already prepared. Instead of being driven to the life of a Pharisee in religion, of laborious and exhausting effort to be saved, he receives salvation as a free gift, a mere gratuity, and is now left free to exercise disinterested (not self-centered, unselfish) benevolence, and to live and labor for the salvation of others, leaving his own soul unreservedly to Jesus Christ as Lord and Savior.

The fact that God has provided and given the believer salvation as a gratuity is calculated to awaken in the believer a concern for others. When he sees them dying for the lack of salvation, he wants them to be brought to the knowledge of the truth and be saved. How far from every selfish motive are the gospel influences! The gospel exhibits God, not as the law exhibits God, as an irreconcilable enemy, but as a grieved and offended Father, willing to be reconciled, more so, very desirous that His subjects should become reconciled to Him and live. This is calculated to beget love. It exhibits God as making the greatest sacrifice to reconcile sinners to Him; and from no other motive than a pure and disinterested (not self-centered, unselfish) regard to their happiness. Try this in your own family. The law represents God as armed with wrath, and determined to punish the sinner, without hope or help. The gospel represents God as offended, indeed, yet so anxious that sinners should return to Him, that He has made the greatest conceivable sacrifices out of pure disinterested love to His wandering children.

I once heard a father say that he had tried in his family to imitate the government of God. When his child did wrong, he reasoned with him and showed him his faults. When he was fully convinced and confounded and condemned, so that he had not a word to say, then the father asked him, "Do you deserve to be punished?" "Yes, Sir," he replied. The father would then say, "I know it. Now, if I were to let you go, what influence would that have over the other children? Rather than let you go without being punished, I will take the punishment myself." The father laid the ferule* on himself, and it had the most astonishing effect on the mind of his child. He had never tried anything so perfectly subduing to the child's mind than this. From the laws of mind, it must be so. It affects the mind in a manner entirely different from the naked law.

Justification by faith brings the mind under an entirely new set of influences, and leaves it free to weigh the reasons for holiness and decide accordingly. Under the law, none but motives of hope and fear can operate on the sinner's mind. Under the gospel, the influence of hope and fear are set aside, and the mind thinks about a new set of considerations. The gospel gives a view of God's entire loving character. It gives the most heart-breaking sin-subduing views of God.

Justification by faith presents God to the senses and exhibits God's disinterestedness**. Satan prevailed against our first parents by leading them to doubt God's disinterestedness. The gospel demonstrates the truth and corrects this lie. The law represents God as the inexorable enemy of the sinner, as securing happiness to all who will perfectly obey, but thundering down wrath on all who disobey. The gospel reveals new features in God's character, not known before. Doubtless, the gospel increases the love of all holy beings, and gives greater joy to the angels in heaven, greatly increasing their love and confidence and admiration, when they see God's amazing pity and forbearance toward the guilty. The law drove the devils to hell, and it drove Adam and Eve from Paradise. However, when the blessed spirits see the same holy God waiting on rebels and opening His heart and giving His beloved Son for them; then, taking such unwearied pains for thousands of years to save sinners, do you think it has no influence in strengthening the motives in their minds to obedience and love?

The devil, who is a purely selfish being, is always accusing others of being selfish. He accused Job of this, "Doth Job fear God for naught?" (Job 1:9—KJV). He accused God to our first parents of being selfish, and that the only reason for His forbidding them to eat of the tree of knowledge was the fear that they might come to know as much as himself. The gos-

5

Romans 3:31

pel shows what God is. If God were selfish, He would not take such pains to save those whom He might with perfect ease crush to hell. Nothing is so calculated to make selfish persons ashamed of their selfishness, as to see disinterested benevolence in others. Hence, the wicked are always trying to appear disinterested. Let the selfish individual who has any heart see true benevolence in others and it is like coals of fire on his head. The wise man understood this when he said, "If thine enemy hunger, feed him; and if he is thirsty, give him drink; for in so doing thou shalt heap coals of fire on his head (Romans 12:20—KJV). Nothing is so calculated to cut down an enemy, win him over, and make him a friend than living according to the gospel of God.

The gospel of Jesus Christ shows sinners that, notwithstanding all that they have done to God, God still exercises disinterested love toward them. When the sinner sees God stooping from heaven to save him, and understands that it is indeed TRUE, O how it melts and breaks down the heart and strikes a deathblow to selfishness. The gospel wins the sinner over to unbounded confidence in God and holy love. God has so constituted the mind that it must necessarily do homage to virtue. It must do this as long as it retains the powers of moral agency. This is as true in hell as in heaven. The devil feels this. When an individual sees that God has no interested (selfish) motives to condemn him, when he sees that God offers salvation as a mere gratuity through faith, he cannot but feel admiration for God's benevolence. His selfishness is crushed and the law has done its work. He sees that all his selfish endeavors have done no good, and the next step is for his heart to go out in disinterested love.

Suppose a person was under sentence of death for rebellion, and had tried many expedients to recommend himself to the government, but failed, because they were all hollow-hearted and selfish. He sees that the government understands his motives, and that he is not really reconciled to his government. He knows himself that they were all hypocritical and selfish endeavors, moved by the hope of favor or the fear of wrath, and that the government is more and more incensed at his hypocrisy. Just now let a paper be brought to him from the government, offering him a free pardon on the simple condition that he would receive it as a mere gratuity, making no account of his own works—what influence will it have on his mind? The moment he finds the penalty set aside, and that he has no need to go to work by any self-righteous efforts, his mind is filled with admiration. Now, let it appear that the government has made the greatest sacrifices to procure this, and his selfishness is slain, and he melts down like a child at his sovereign's feet. He is ready to obey the law because he loves his sovereign.

All true obedience turns on faith. Faith secures all the requisite influences to produce sanctification. Faith gives the doctrines of eternity access to the mind and a hold on the heart. In this world, the motives of time are addressed to the senses. The motives that influence the spirits of the just in heaven do not reach us through the senses. However, when a believer exercises faith, the wall is broken down, and the vast realities of eternity act on the mind here with the same kind of influence that they have in eternity. Mind is mind, everywhere. Moreover, were it not for the darkness of unbelief, people would live here just as they do in the eternal world. Sinners here would rage and blaspheme, just as they do in hell. Saints would love, obey, and praise God, just as they do in heaven. Now, faith makes all these things realities. Faith swings the mind loose from the clogs of the world and the believer beholds God, and apprehends His law and His love. In no other way can these motives take hold on the mind. What a mighty action must it have on the mind, when it takes hold of the love of Christ! What a life-giving power, when the pure motives of the gospel crowd into the mind and stir it up with energy divine! Every Christian knows that in proportion to the strength of his faith, his mind is buoyant and active. When his faith flags, his soul is dark and listless. Faith alone places the things of time and eternity in their true comparison, and sets down the things of time and sense at their real value. Faith breaks up the delusions of the mind; the soul shakes itself free from its errors and clogs and rises up in communion with God.

REMARKS

It is as unphilosophical as it is unscriptural to attempt to convert and sanctify the minds of sinners without the motives of the gospel. You may press the sinner with the law, and make him see his own character, the

5

Romans 3:31

greatness and justice of God, and his ruined condition; however, hide the motives of the gospel from his mind, and it is all in vain.

It is absurd to think that the offers of the gospel are calculated to beget a selfish hope. Some are afraid to throw out upon the sinner's mind all the character of God. They try to make him submit to God by casting him down in despair. This is not only against the gospel, but it is absurd in itself. It is absurd to think that in order to destroy the selfishness of a sinner, you must hide from him the knowledge of how much God loves and pities him, and what great sacrifices he has made to save him.

It is far from being true that sinners are in danger of getting false hopes if they are allowed to know the real compassion of God. Without showing them the real compassion of God, it is impossible to give them any other than a false hope. Withholding from the sinner who is writhing under conviction of sin the fact that God has provided salvation as a mere gratuity is the very way to confirm his selfishness; and, if he gets any hope, it must be a false one. To press him to submission by the law alone is to set him to build a self-righteous foundation.

As far as we can see, salvation by grace (which is not bestowed in any degree for our own works) is the only possible way of reclaiming selfish beings. Suppose salvation was not altogether gratuitous, but that some degree of good works was taken into the account, and for those good works in part we were justified—just so far as this consideration is in the mind, just so far there is a stimulus to selfishness. You must bring the sinner to see that he is entirely dependent on free grace; that a full and complete justification is bestowed on the first act of faith, as a mere gratuity and no part of it as an equivalent for anything he is to do. This alone dissolves the influence of selfishness and secures holy action.

Because this is true, we should give sinners the fullest possible possession in the speediest manner the whole plan of salvation. They should be made to see the law, and their own guilt, and that they have no way to save themselves. Then, the whole length and breadth and height and depth of the love of God should be opened more fully to them. If you present the plan of salvation fully, you will more effectually crush his selfishness and subdue his soul in love to God. Do not be afraid, when conversing with sinners, to show the whole plan of salvation and give the fullest possible exhibition of the infinite compassion of God. Show him that, notwith-standing his guilt, the Son of God is knocking at the door and beseeching him to be reconciled to God.

You see why so many convicted sinners continue so long compassing Mount Sinai with self-righteous efforts to save themselves by their own works. How often you find sinners trying to get more feeling, or waiting until they have made more prayers and greater efforts, and expecting to recommend themselves to God in this way. You need to drive the sinner from this thinking and make him see that he is all the while looking for salvation under the law. He must see that all this is superseded by the gospel offering him all he wants as a mere gratuity. He must hear Jesus saying to him, "Ye will not come unto me that ye may have life! O no, you are willing to pray, and go to meeting, and read the Bible, or anything, but come unto me. Sinner, this is the road. I am the way, the truth, and the life. No man cometh to the Father but by me. I am the resurrection and the life. I am the light of the world. Here, sinner, is what you want. Instead of trying your self-righteous prayers and efforts, here is what you are looking for, only believe and you shall be saved."

Do you see why so many who profess to be Christians are always in the dark? They are looking at their sins, confining their observations to them-selves, and losing sight of the fact that they have only to take right hold of Jesus Christ and throw themselves upon Him, and all is well.

The law is useful to convict sinners of their sin and guilt; but, in fact, it never breaks the heart. The gospel alone does that. The degree in which a convert is broken hearted is in proportion to the degree of clearness with which he apprehends the gospel.

"Converts," if you can call those who entertain a hope under legal preaching, may have an intellectual approbation of the law, and a sort of dry zeal, but they never make mellow, brokenhearted Christians. If they have not seen God in the attitude in which He is exhibited in the gospel, they are not such Christians as those you will see sometimes, who have tears trembling in their eyes and bodies shaking with emotion at the name of Jesus.

Do you see what to do with sinners who are under conviction of sin? Do you know what to say to those who profess to be Christians but are in darkness. You must lead them right to Christ. Encourage them to take hold of the plan of salvation by faith. It is vain to expect that you can lead them to saving faith and do them good in any other way.***

---

*A "ferule" is an instrument that is similar to a flat piece of wood (like a ruler) used to punish children.

**Theologically and philosophically, in the Eighteenth and Nineteenth Centuries, the term "Disinterestedness" meant "the quality of being objective or impartial." It did not mean, as it has come to mean today, "to regard something with no interest or concern." Finney taught that God does not enforce His moral law for any selfish or egocentric reasons. God makes Justification by Faith possible to believers without any partiality or selfish motivation on His part. God's offer of Justification by Faith and the gospel plan of salvation proves God's disinterested love and shows that God is not Self-centered or selfish.

*** Charles G. Finney, "The Oberlin Evangelist," 1837, *Lectures to Professing Christians*, 1880, 307–319, *Principles of Victory*, 46–54. For Review: Answer the Study Questions on page 176, Cowles page 195.

6

The Foundation, Conditions, Relations, and Results of Faith

1850

What shall we say then that Abraham our father, as pertaining to the flesh, hath found? For if Abraham were justified by works, he hath whereof to glory; but not before God. For what saith the scripture? Abraham believed God, and it was counted unto him for righteousness. Now to him that worketh is the reward not reckoned of grace, but of debt. But to him that worketh not, but believeth on him that justifieth the ungodly, his faith is counted for righteousness. —Romans 4:1-5—KJV

What then shall we say that Abraham, our forefather, discovered in this matter? If, in fact, Abraham was justified by works, he had something to boast about—but not before God. What does the Scripture say? "Abraham believed God, and it was credited to him as righteousness." Now when a man works, his wages are not credited to him as a gift, but as an obligation. However, to the man who does not work but trusts God who justifies the wicked, his faith is credited as righteousness. —Romans 4:1-5—NIV

The passage in Genesis 15, refers to Abraham—to the promises God had made to him—to his faith in those promises, and to the Lord's acceptance of that faith. These topics are first brought to our view in Genesis 12, again in Genesis 17, and thenceforward frequently in the course of Abraham's history. The case was highly instructive, and Saint Paul could not fail to see its important bearings. Hence, Saint Paul makes free use of Abraham's faith as an illustration of both faith and its results. It is important for us to notice the foundation of Abraham's faith, some conditions of faith, faith's governmental relations, and its natural relations and results.

The foundation of faith.

The foundation of Abraham's faith was not anything whatever in himself. It was not the fact, either real or supposed, that he had been himself converted. There is no intimation that he ever so much as thought about whether he had been converted. He exercised his faith irrespective of any opinions or thoughts on this question. Nor did his faith rest on the assumption that he was himself in a right state of mind. He did not, as far as we can see, assume this, and thereupon ground his confidence that God would do for him what He had promised. Nor did his faith rest in the confidence he might have had in his own integrity of character. There is not the least intimation of this.

Abraham's faith rested on God's veracity and devotion to the truth. It does not appear that Abraham took into view anything else whatever as a ground of his faith except the simple veracity of God. He simply relied on what God had said because God said it. God met him and told him certain things; Abraham believed them, although they were apparently impossible. It was enough for him that God had said so. He rested in God as a being of veracity and truthfulness.

The conditions of faith.

Very commonly, people confuse the conditions of faith with faith itself. This is a fundamental mistake. For example, the rational recognition of God's natural and moral attributes is a condition of faith, but is not by any means faith itself. Unless a person sees and knows that God possesses the moral attributes ascribed to Him, he can see no ground for rational confidence in Him. How could Abraham have had confidence in God, if he had not believed in His natural and moral attributes? He must have believed this, or he could not rationally believe that God would and could fulfill His promises.

Especially note, as a condition of faith, Abraham must have had confidence in God's moral attributes. He must have believed that God is good; for of necessity you must intellectually apprehend this attribute of the divine character before your mind can rationally believe that God will certainly fulfill His promises. Hence, distinguishing between the conditions of faith and faith itself is fundamental. One might intellectually apprehend these attributes as clearly as an angel in heaven does, and yet not have gospel faith.

Another condition of faith is the promise of God. It would not have been virtue in Abraham to believe that God would grant him a son, or give his posterity the land of Canaan, if God had never promised to do so. God first revealed His covenant with Abraham, and connected with it precious promises; then, a condition was fulfilled for faith on Abraham's part—then, but not before. In the same way, the covenant of grace, clearly apprehended, as revealed by God, is a condition of saving faith now. When God in any way reveals the substance of this covenant—whether through dim types and prophecies as before Christ came, or in the broad blaze of gospel day as when He actually came, then the way is opened for the intelligent and acceptable exercise of gospel faith. No doubt, Adam and Eve received sufficient revelation from God to lay a foundation for their faith. Eve obviously understood from the promise given in Genesis 3:15 that salvation from the power of Satan was to come through her posterity; for at the birth of Cain, her firstborn, she seems to have supposed that this was the promised seed. In this particular case, she was indeed mistaken, but not in her faith that God would bring salvation through her posterity. Plainly, both Adam and Eve received and believed at this time the revelations of divine mercy. The Lord was exceedingly kind toward them in His mode of convicting them of their first and great sin.

6

Romans 4:1-5

81

How beautiful and how gracious that He should himself clothe them to hide the shame of their nakedness! How significant too that this clothing should be of skins—of skins, which almost beyond question God took from animals now for the first time slain for a sacrifice! It seems most fitting that here for the first time the idea of sacrifice should be developed, and the human race be taught in the persons of Adam and Eve, that "almost all things are by the law purged with blood; and without shedding of blood is no remission" (Hebrews 9:22—KJV). A most expressive and beautiful type! What could more forcibly express displeasure against sin—grace toward the real sinner—and the substitution of an innocent victim in place of the guilty, as a ground for the grace shown the latter!

Another condition of this governmental justification is that the sinner believes. The simple belief of this record, the heart yielding itself up to the control of the truth believed—this is the condition on which the full blessings of Christ's work are conferred to him.

In the case of Abraham, faith gave him, as indeed it does all believers, the full benefit of all the work comprised in the death and resurrection of the Lord Jesus. All that Christ has done for the sinner becomes his on condition of his embracing it by faith. This is the only condition. Abraham was to believe the promise before Christ actually came. All believers since Christ's death are to believe on Christ as actually come. In each case the condition is substantially the same, it is believing what God has said, and taking hold of His promise to rely upon it as truth.

God revealed the covenant of grace to Abraham yet more fully than to Adam and Eve. To Abraham, God expanded more distinctly His purposes of loving-kindness toward a sinning race, and He made yet more distinct and definite the ground of saving faith. Never forget! *The ultimate ground of the sinner's justification is God's great and pure love.* In love alone, the whole plan of salvation had its origin in the mind of God. In love alone, God executed His plan and sent His Son as our Savior.

The governmental relations of saving faith.

We need to consider the governmental relations of saving faith. For, example, what relations did Abraham's faith sustain to the government of

God? Scripture answers by saying, "And he believed in the LORD; and he counted it to him for righteousness" (Genesis 15:6—KJV). His faith was set down—passed to his account, as righteousness—as if it were perfect obedience. Those in business will understand this phrase so current in their pecuniary transactions. A credit passed to a person's account—a receipt in full—accounted as full payment of his debt. The obvious meaning seems to be that God accepted Abraham's faith instead of that perfect obedience which had been before required. All people having fallen into sin and hence having come under condemnation, God passes to their credit the righteousness of Christ, as if Christ had passed to their credit in the bank of heaven enough to cancel all of their debt.

The term "righteousness," as used in this connection, denotes "justification." This is its proper meaning. God accepted Abraham's faith in Him in the place of perfect obedience as the ground of His pardon. Thus pardoned, God can treat the sinner as if he had not sinned. He had sinned, indeed, but under the economy of grace, God treats him governmentally as if he had not sinned. Governmentally, God regards him as perfect. By this, I do not mean that the law did not regard him as a sinner, for it did so regard him, and could not do otherwise. It could not blot from its tablets the record of his past sins, but God could, so to speak, pass to his credit the faith he had exercised, which is accounted to him for righteousness. For this reason, the Law-giver can treat him not as sinful, but as righteous.

Yet, do not lose sight of this: providentially, he may be and is still treated as a sinner. Under the providential, disciplinary government of God, he is regarded as a sinner—still, imperfect and needing discipline to improve his character and train him for heaven. Hence, while governmentally he is regarded as righteous and not doomed to hell, yet providentially, it is not forgotten that he has sinned, and that he still needs discipline to evolve and perfect the spirit and the habits of holiness.

The results of saving faith.

Finally, consider the natural relations and results of faith. Faith is naturally connected with obedience. Faith stands related to obedience by its very nature. Faith is confidence in God's veracity. As a result, faith naturally leads the soul to obey all God's requirements.

Cases sometimes occur in which we may get from our own observation very striking and just views of the nature of faith, psychologically considered. You may sometimes see people give themselves up to another so completely as to believe everything they say, and be entirely controlled by their influence. I was much struck with this in the course of the Second Advent discussions. Some seemed most manifestly to have unbounded confidence in all Mr. Miller said and believed.* Often they manifested a similar confidence in their sub-leaders.

I also once heard a man say—a man who I have reason to fear is a wicked man, "That woman will do just what I tell her to do, and I can make her believe anything I say." He said this in her presence, and I had but too much reason to think that it was literally true.

I once felt constrained to say to one lady, "I am afraid you will go to destruction. You have given yourself up to be led anywhere, and I do greatly fear this will not end short of plunging you in absolute ruin. You believe the most utter nonsense as strongly and firmly as if God himself had met you and told you to believe it."

These cases may serve to illustrate the natural results of faith. Let a person commit himself to another as a leader and teacher, and the latter can lead him anywhere and any way he pleases. Let a soldier commit himself thus to his general; he can then be led right into the very jaws of death. So let confidence be cherished in another; its natural result will be to bring the confiding mind under the complete dominion of the mind confided in.

Such was the natural influence of Abraham's faith. We see him hanging upon what God said, just like a child upon its parent. If anything happened to try him, we see him coming forth from the trial in the utmost simplicity of character. How beautiful and how noble to see him stand firm as a rock while the storms of temptation dash around his feet! So it is with real faith always. Abraham's faith had in it nothing peculiar in character or in results. It was simple faith—nothing more.

Faith naturally results in joy and peace. The things believed are such that the mind cannot but feel the highest joy and the most quiet repose.

If you really understand and believe what God says, why not feel at rest? What more does God need to say to inspire confidence in Him? Who does not know that the confidence in One believed to be able to save to the uttermost must assuredly inspire the rest of sweet repose—the joy of unalloyed confidence and trust? Truly, God has said everything we need to have said to make us feel that His promised protection is round about us as the mountains are round about Jerusalem. Has He not told us that His everlasting arms are underneath us evermore? Can we ever sink, sustained by such supports? Who does not know that simply to believe in all this naturally results in peace, quietness, and assurance forever? Who does not see that these results flow as naturally as any other results flow from their appropriate cause? Who can believe this good news and not be greatly glad? Is not that joy both intense and abiding which springs from peace, deep and broad as a river, and from a righteousness which flows and rolls its mountain waves as the sea?

Faith in Jesus Christ overcomes the world. By this, I mean that it overcomes the influence of the world upon the mind. Let a person believe what the Bible teaches about the future state, and he will deem it a small thing to be judged of human judgment. But, O! To stand right in the eye of the Great and Final Judge—this will be his supreme concern. Let him only be assured of this, and all within is peace and joy. Let him only apprehend God's universal providence and put his trust in this all-present and all-controlling Deity; then, all is peace and joy. Whether sick or well, it is all the same. Nothing disturbs his peace, for he knows that under God's hand all things shall work together for his good. No matter whether he has much or little of earthly supply, he knows that he has just so much as is good for him, for the amount is wisely and kindly measured out to him by One who both knows and loves him. He may enjoy honor or dishonor. He may have much learning or none. All is well, if he knows that God has appointed all just as it is, and if he can thoroughly trust it all to be perfectly right. Be the circumstances what they may, he knows that what is infinitely wise and good is taking place and always will be. Now he has only to believe this, and it is all the same to him whether he has little, or much, or none at all of this world's good things. If he will only believe with unfaltering faith that all is wise and well, he has a key in his

6

Romans 4:1-5

own bosom with which he can unlock all treasures.

Imagine a person professing to be a Christian under God's glorious government fretting about a pin! Alas! What is the matter? He has lost a single pin! This is not the worst thing—he has lost his faith! I saw him one day in great trouble and anxiety of mind. It was a few days after his conversion, and then he seemed a bright and joyful convert; but he lost his way and fell into temptation. Alas! Go and ask him now what is the matter. "I have lost my Jesus!" It is well that he knows it. Many do not seem to know it when the fact is most obvious to everybody else. Listen to the Psalmist, and notice the beauty and pertinence of his words. He sinks into the deep mire of the Slough of Despond**; yet opening his eyes somewhat to his condition, he cries out, "Why art thou cast down, O my soul, and why art thou disquieted within me? Hope thou in God, for I shall yet praise him" (Psalm 42:5—KJV). He would excite his own soul to believe God; hence, he begins to arraign and catechize himself for his causeless unbelief: "O my soul, Why art thou cast down? Believe thou in God! Believe what? Believe in God. Believe that thou shalt still praise Him."

Faith naturally overcomes the flesh. If a person has faith, why shall he go about to gratify his appetites? Shall he make their gratification his chief good? No. Truly, he will understand that the kingdom of heaven is not meat and drink. If you see a man given up to the indulgence of his appetites, you see an unbeliever. You see one who does not apprehend the great things of the eternal world as living and all-controlling realities. He is under the dominion of his flesh. Faith breaks up this dominion and asserts its own in its stead. What has faith to do with sensuality? What communion is there between light and darkness? What concord is there between Christ and Belial? Just the same as between faith and sensuality. Faith overcomes Satan. One who believes God knows that Satan is a liar and the father of lies. Without faith, you are Satan's dupe, Satan's slave, Satan's drudge; but faith in Jesus Christ emancipates your soul from the dominion of his lies.

REMARKS

The faith of Abraham was purely a mental act. The apostle speaks of it curiously. "If Abraham were justified by works, he would have whereof to glory; but not before God" (Romans 4:2—KJV). He has nothing of which to glory; therefore, he is not justified by works. Plainly, he was not justified at all by works in the Jewish sense. It was not on the ground of certain external doings, but on the ground of his mental faith that he was justified. The purely mental act of faith was the condition, itself antecedent to all external manifestations and the condition of them. This faith is accounted to him for righteousness.

Some confound the condition of faith with faith itself. Some just knowledge of God is doubtless an indispensable condition to the exercise of faith; but this knowledge—this intellectual apprehension of God—is not to be confounded with faith itself.

Some look to something within themselves as the ground of faith. Consequently, they attend continually to their own mental states instead of looking up to God. They are evermore looking within at their state of feeling for evidence upon which they are to believe. Believe what? Not believe in themselves, but believe in God. Under the pretense of self-examination, they are forever playing the fool with themselves, and looking down, as they suppose, into the depths of their hearts to find evidence on which to believe. God announces to them a truth, and says, "Believe." They reply, "I can believe that, if I can only get the evidence that I am in a right state of mind." But what is a right state of mind? A state of faith! Believing is the right exercise; nothing else is right. The great piety of Abraham explained in the Bible is simple belief—trust: this constitutes a right state of mind. He believed what God said, not on the ground of having certain right emotions and feelings, but because it was God who had said it. What if Abraham had said, "O, I could believe all God has said, if I only had the evidence"? Of what? Do you want evidence that God is true? No, but I want evidence that I am in a right state of mind. Abraham was not such a fool as to back out of God's light into the darkness of his own mind and draw a veil of thick darkness over and all around about him. No, it was enough for him that God had spoken, and that God was true.

From reading the Bible, it really seems as if God was unable to say any thing to Abraham that Abraham would not believe. God almost seemed

6

Romans 4:1-5

to tell him lies to try his faith, but Abraham would believe. The Lord told him he should have a son; but still he went on in His providence as if He never meant to fulfill His promise. Continually, God seemed to contradict His promises. After Isaac was born and grown, He told Abraham to take him far away to a specified mountain, and there kill him! O, what a scene was that! Yet Abraham believed God. He knew that God could even raise his Isaac from the dead; hence, why should he fear to obey God, even when He gave such a command? If this man of God were among us in our prayer meetings, would he do as some now do—be looking continually after his feelings? No! He would simply believe God.

Yet, notice how sorely God tried him. "Take now," said God, "thy son, thine only son Isaac," (how every word sinks to the bottom of a parent's heart!). Take him away from his loved home, and from his fond mother—forever! (Genesis 22:2—KJV). Set off on this dreadful expedition tomorrow. One night intervened. Did the tried father sleep quietly as ever that night? If he did, it must have been the rest of faith. In the morning he rose, and said not a word to Sarah. He could not have her sympathy, for (probably) he could not trust her faith against her maternal feelings. His own faith stood apparently unfaltering. The simplicity of his faith was the glory of his piety.

Abraham had but few things to believe. If those full revelations made to us had been made to him, what a mighty, triumphant life he must have lived! In what a sunset of glory he must have died! Only a single ray fell from heaven upon his eye, yet his eye caught this one ray, and his heart believed. On that ray of truth, he kept his eye fixed continually. O, if he were to live now and among us, what would he think of our faith? What could he think of us, always prating over our unbelief as if we had not faith enough to keep us above the fear of hell!

By what they say, many who profess to be Christians greatly confuse young converts. They seem not to have gone a step beyond babyhood. They are no more able to stand alone than a mere child, though counting the years of their church life, they ought for the time spent be of adult age and adult strength.

When a young convert sets out in the Christian life with a flood of emotions and these soon subside, it sometimes happens that he falls into deep trouble. Like a raw hand aboard ship, he shows but too soon that he is no sailor. A storm comes on, the mountain waves dash high—such a wind he never knew before—his knees smite together, and he cries out, "Alas! I am lost, I am lost!" Likewise, the timid convert feels when he thinks he has lost his Jesus. The fact is he has only lost his faith. Perhaps this sad loss has befallen him because much older Christians, who should have strengthened his faith rather than weakened it, misguided him.

How plain it is that God meant to confirm our faith and teach us to keep it always strong and earnest. Else, why did He give us such a history as this of Abraham? Look at this man of living faith! See him pushing his way along with only one dim ray of light, yet firm as a rock amid the waves; steadfast, though all around be dark as death. But O, what a zigzag course many now pursue! Faltering now, and now turning aside to shun the lions in the way; feeling their path along as if they could not trust the Mighty One who has said, "This is the way; go forward, and fear not, for I am with thee." How many such Christians would it take to promote a revival? Ten thousand of them would not promote one! In fact, the more there are, the worse for the cause of God; the greater the difficulties in promoting revivals where their influence is felt. O how weak and sickly they are! They need to be fed with a spoon like an infant. You might just as soon march an army of invalids against Gibraltar, as lead such Christians out to conflict by prayer and faith in promoting revivals of the Christian faith. I can afford and endure to see infancy and weakness in young converts; but when I see old Christians still shut up to the diet and leading-strings of infants, it is so afflictive, so disheartening! To see them go around and around forever in a circle after their feelings, their feelings. What an abomination that they do not learn to walk by faith! A perfect state of the physical system does not make a man think much about his health. It leaves him to mind his appropriate business and seek the proper enjoyments of life. If his digestion is good, he never thinks of his stomach. Why should he? Perhaps he never knows from any sensations felt that he has any stomach. However, if his digestion is bad, then alas! The poor man has enough to do in thinking of his troubled stomach. So of the sickly Christian. You see him perpetually troubled about his feelings, his feelings, like the invalid who runs to the glass to see his tongue! O when will such Christians learn to have faith, and be strong in the Mighty God of Jacob.

A most unhealthy religion is forever dwelling on views and frames and feelings. How is it in heaven? Are they thinking of their feelings and frames? No. They are so absorbed in the great objects before them that they are unconscious of the lapse of time. Perhaps a thousand of our years may pass over them and leave no consciousness of its having been a moment. Is this extravagant? No. Have you not been sometimes so engrossed that you could not mark the lapse of time at all? We mark time by noticing the succession of events. Have you not been so much engrossed as not at all to notice this succession? I recollect the case of a young convert in the northern part of New York State, who on one occasion prayed all night. When he came to consciousness of time and began to think what time it was, he was astonished to find it morning!

It is said of William Tennant that once he rode all day in thought so profound that he never knew until he reached the end of his journey that he had been bleeding profusely at the nose.*** Now in such cases, their own state is not the subject of thought at all. They are far indeed from studying and watching over their own feelings.

This latter is, as I have said, a most unhealthy state. He who is forever dwelling upon his own spiritual frames, instead of being absorbed in the objects of faith, is a poor, spiritual dyspeptic, suffering from spiritual indigestion. This thinking of his own frames is the very thing which destroys his religion.

Suppose I go to England and leave my wife at home. Far away from her, I set myself to examine my feelings to see if I love my wife. I turn my mind away from her, and fasten it upon my love. I make this love the only and the all-absorbing subject of my thought. What will be the result? Who does not know that the affection of love is correlated to its object? In this case, my affection is correlated to my wife and cannot spring up and develop itself except in view of its object. Hence, I must think of my wife, if I would make it possible for the affection of love to develop itself. Contemplation of the object is the condition of all manifestation of the affections. Consequently, by turning my mind wholly away from the object, and then demanding that love to that object should manifest itself,

I demand a natural impossibility. Let me do this and I might pronounce myself a stark hypocrite, and be as well employed as many "Christians" are who withhold their contemplations from God and all the proper objects of faith, and exercise themselves in scanning and trying to judge of their feelings. O what misguided efforts are these!****

---

* William Miller was born February 15, 1782, in Pittsfield, Massachusetts, and died December 20, 1849, in Low Hampton, New York. He founded and led a movement called "Millerism" and his followers were called "Millerites." He taught that the Second Coming of Christ was imminent. In 1831, he began to preach that the world would end about the year 1843. He was wrong, and Finney noted that Miller had deceived many. Finney preached this sermon only a couple of months following Miller's death.

** Finney may be referring to the "Slough of Despond" described in John Bunyan's *Pilgrim's Progress*. Other than the Bible, by Finney's time more copies of *Pilgrim's Progress* had been printed and read than any other Christian book.

6

Romans 4:1-5

"The Slough of Despond" in *Pilgrim's Progress*

Now I saw in my dream that, just as they had ended this talk, they drew near to a very miry slough that was in the midst of the plain; and they being heedless, did both fall suddenly into the bog. The name of the slough was "Despond." Here, therefore, they wallowed for a time, being grievously bedaubed with the dirt; and CHRISTIAN, because of the burden that was on his back, began to sink in the mire. [Editor's Note: This burden was his sins.]

Pliable. Then said PLIABLE, "Ah! neighbour CHRISTIAN, where are you now?"

Christian. "Truly," said CHRISTIAN, "I do not know."

Pliable. At that PLIABLE began to be offended, and he angrily said to his fellow, "Is this the happiness you have told me of all this while? If we have such ill speed at our first setting out, what may we expect 'twixt this and our journey's end? If I get out again with my life, you shall possess the brave country alone." And with that he gave a desperate struggle or two, and got out of the mire on that side of the slough which was next to his own house: so away he went, and CHRISTIAN saw him no more.

Wherefore CHRISTIAN was left to tumble in the Slough of Despond alone; but still he endeavoured to struggle to that side of the slough that was farthest from his own house, and next to the wicket gate: which he did, but could not get out, because of the burden that was upon his back.... (Then, HELP told CHRISTIAN:)

"This miry slough is such a place as cannot be mended: it is the descent whither the scum and filth that attends conviction for sin doth continually run; and therefore it is called the Slough of Despond. For still, as the sinner is awakened about his lost condition, there arises in his soul many fears and doubts, and discouraging apprehensions, which all of them get together, and settle in this place: and this is the reason of the badness of this ground."

*** William Tennant was a Presbyterian revival preacher and educator, who was a graduate of the University of Edinburgh. In 1726, he founded an academy, "the Log College," to educate ministers. Prior to his death in 1746, the College had graduated 16 to 18 ministers.

**** Charles G. Finney, "The Oberlin Evangelist," February 13, 1850, *Principles of Liberty*, 37–45. In *Principles of Righteousness*, I have added "Results" to the original title. For Review: Answer the Study Questions on page 177, Cowles page 196.

7

The Rationality of Faith
1851

He staggered not at the promise of God through unbelief; but was strong in faith, giving glory to God; And being fully persuaded that, what he had promised, he was able also to perform. —Romans 4:20-21—KJV

Yet he did not waver through unbelief regarding the promise of God, but was strengthened in his faith and gave glory to God, being fully persuaded that God had power to do what he had promised. —Romans 4:20-21—NIV

These words were spoken of Abraham, as you will see by reading the context in which they are found. Faith is the heart's confidence in God. This is faith in its generic form. Its specific form relates to particular things—belief in the promises, in Christ, in the doctrines of the Bible, and in all the various assertions that God makes in His word. This specific form of faith differs from faith in its generic or simple form, which implies a general confidence in the existence, attributes, and character of God. The mind's resting in these things is faith; that is, faith

93

in its simple form. Take special notice of this: faith in God is not a mere assent to these things or a mere intellectual conviction that they are true. Faith is the heart, and the mind, and the will, resting in this truth—that God is and that He possesses certain attributes and character. Faith in its specific form is the belief of the heart in certain declarations of God; a belief in His wisdom and goodness, in His assertions respecting Christ, and in everything that He has said and promised. Faith develops itself in a great many specific forms, but the root of it is heart confidence in God himself.

Tests of faith.

We need to discuss some things in the word of God that test the faith of finite minds. We also need to see how faith disposes of these things; and that true faith is not subdued and overcome by considering these things. There is a great purpose to trials of faith. When people, who profess to believe, stumble or stagger at these things, they consequently and by natural necessity lose the blessing that God intends for those who maintain true faith.

One of the things that tries the faith of God's creatures, and is very common and most striking, is the existence of so much evil and misery in this world. God declares that He is acquainted with all. He affirms that He is omnipotent, omniscient, and everywhere present. God knows all things and is all-powerful. He declares himself infinitely good, and is disposed to do good. Now, that under the government of such a Being as this there should be so much evil, and so much that is sinful, and so much misery—as a matter of fact we know there is—is greatly calculated to challenge the faith of people. That these evil things should exist, and be everywhere observable in this world to an immense extent, is to many minds so great a mystery, so difficult to reconcile with the existence and declared attributes of God, that they stumble and even call in question the fact that there is a God at all.

By the way, another thing that God asserts, and that reason affirms, is the existence of a providence that guides and controls all events. God has a design in everything that He does. At the very beginning, God had a design. In all that God does, He is pursuing this design to its accomplishment; and this design proceeds from a being who is infinitely good and infinitely wise.

Now the existence of evil in the world does not seem to harmonize with the things that God says of himself—with His wisdom and goodness—many minds therefore find great difficulty in getting over these facts. Understand, it is not at present my design to explain this, but simply to notice the facts at which unbelievers stumble, and which are calculated to try the faith of God's creatures. The introduction of sin into this world and its existence in the world is greatly calculated to test the faith of the most holy being in the universe. There is little doubt that the angels were unable to comprehend for a time why God allowed such a state of things to be. God's reason for all this may have gradually developed in their minds, but at first the difficulty could have only been overcome by faith—how this is done I shall observe later.

Doctrinal obstacles to belief.

But let me say again that the manner in which the Bible reveals God is also a great stumbling-block to many. The doctrine of the Trinity, for example, is an obstacle to belief for a great many because they cannot understand it, any better than they can understand a great many other things. Because they cannot understand it, they reject it. They say that it cannot be, and so they will not receive it simply because they cannot explain it. Just so with respect to the incarnation of the Son of God; because they cannot understand how humanity and Deity could be united, they reject the doctrine and will not believe it. Now, we admit at once, there is no occasion for denying it, and to do so would be as absurd as it is unnecessary, that these doctrines are very mysterious. But they are announced as facts, that God was in Christ, that Christ was both God and man. Of course, we readily admit that this declaration is a great trial to the faith of finite creatures; but then, God made the announcement himself and He ought to be believed. The doctrine of the atonement is another obstacle to some; that God should give His own Son to die for sinners, and that He should actually suffer, is a difficulty that can only be

7

Romans 4:20-21

overcome by faith—unbelief will suggest a multitude of difficulties and reject God's word.

The doctrine of the resurrection, the doctrine of justification by faith, the doctrine of sanctification by faith, and all the other doctrines of the Bible are obstacles to the minds of some. Individuals who find no difficulties in them have no faith, and show that they have not well considered them; but however difficult they may be, there is ten thousand times greater absurdity in disbelieving them than in exercising faith in them, because they are based on the testimony of God himself. Nevertheless, unbelief finds great difficulty in admitting them. The mind that has no confidence in God refuses to believe, because it cannot explain how these things all are—of course, such a mind will stumble and stagger at every step.

The manner in which sin was introduced into the world is also a great obstacle to belief for those who have no confidence in God. They will not rest upon the revealed fact unless they can explain it. Of course, if they cannot receive what God says, unless He gives them His reasons for everything that He does, they will find great difficulty in getting along.

Suppose a child should have no confidence in his father, and should therefore want the reasons for his father's conduct in everything that he did. Suppose a child should require his father to explain to him in a satisfactory manner how he did everything before he could believe it. Who cannot see that a family of such unbelievers, stumbling and staggering at every step, would have no confidence in their father at all? If he was conducting a very extensive business on a vast scale, they could not understand as children what even perhaps many people could not comprehend if he explained it to them. How absurd for the children not to put confidence in their father because they could not understand the reasons for all his conduct.

The very greatness of God's promises is often a severe trial to faith. He promises things so great to persons so undeserving—indeed so ill deserving—that unbelief finds it difficult to believe Him, because He says so much and promises so much. The providence of God is often a great trial to faith. How remarkable was the conduct of God toward Abraham, and how greatly calculated to try his faith! He called him out of his father's house, and Abraham obeyed not knowing whither he went. God had reasons in his own mind for his conduct in this matter. God intended to make of Abraham a great nation and through him communicate His will to people. From his family the Savior of sinners should proceed. But God gave Abraham no such intimation of what He was going to do. He called him from his country and told him to go to a certain place that He would show him. After Abraham had obeyed the command, God promised to give him a certain land for a possession and to his seed after him. Although he had no family, God called him and said, "Look toward the heavens and see if you can count the stars for multitude." God promised that his seed should be as numerous as the stars of heaven—and that He would give him the land of Canaan for a possession, and make him the father of many nations. This promise was long and remarkably delayed. Abraham lived in the land that God promised him for a possession only on sufferance. When his wife died, he was obliged to purchase a burial place in that very land that God had promised should be his own—yet we see no signs of any stumbling in his faith. After a long period had elapsed, God promised Abraham that he should have a son by his wife Sarah. Now both Abraham and Sarah were very old. She was long past the age when it was common for women to have children. Nevertheless, Abraham believed that God would do what He had promised. Those who will read and ponder well all the circumstances connected with the trial of Abraham's faith will see that God must have very severely tried his faith. After a long time, this promised son was born. The lad grew—when all at once God takes Abraham by surprise—as He seems always to have done—and says "Take thy son, thine only son, whom thou lovest, and go to a mountain that I will tell thee of, and offer him there for a burnt-offering" (Genesis 22:2—KJV). He not only says to Abraham, "take thy son," but He reminds him that it is his only son, whom he loves; and it is this son, this son of promise, this beloved son, whom he is to offer upon the altar. Now, how infinitely strange is all this; yet Abraham staggered not. He believed that God was able to raise him from the dead. He had such strength of faith that he appears not to have been in much trouble of mind about it. He does not seem even to have revealed to Sarah that he had received any such communication from God. He was so calm

7

Romans 4:20-21

that Sarah did not perceive anything was the matter with him. The next morning he started with his servants to offer Isaac at the place that God was to point out to him. When they came in sight of the place, he caused his servants to wait, lest they should interfere with him when carrying out the command of God. Abraham and his son ascended the mountain where Abraham would offer the sacrifice. Isaac did not understand what his father was going to do. He knew indeed that Abraham was going to offer a burnt-offering, for they had the fire and the wood, but he did not know that he was to be the victim. It did not occur to him at all, for he asked where the lamb was that Abraham intended to offer. So calm was Abraham, that Isaac did not notice anything different in his manner. To the question of his son, Abraham replied, "the Lord will provide himself with a lamb for a burnt offering." When Abraham had prepared the altar, he bound Isaac and laid him on the wood, just as he would have done a lamb. He took the knife, and as he was about to slay his son, God called, and said, "Abraham, Abraham!"—repeating his name rapidly in order to arrest his attention in a moment. "Lay not thy hand upon the lad, neither do thou anything unto him: for now I know that thou fearest God, seeing that thou hast not withheld thy son, thine only son from me." And when Abraham lifted up his eyes, he saw a ram caught in a thicket by his horns, and he offered it instead of his son (Genesis 22:12, 13—KJV). God did this to test the implicitness of Abraham's faith; and this was as plainly manifested as if he had sacrificed his son—for he did do it so far as his mind was concerned. He believed that God would raise him from the dead if sacrificed, for he had no doubt at all that God would fulfill His promise.

Now, this was a beautiful exhibition and illustration of faith. But, let me say, this was exceedingly calculated to try Abraham, as you will perceive. And the manner in which God very often fulfils His promises to people is to them a great obstacle to faith. They are expecting God to fulfill them in one way, and He takes a direct opposite course, which is calculated to subvert all their ideas of things. Now all such things as these are exceedingly calculated to try our faith in God. However, strong faith will not allow itself to stumble at such things. Why should it? Faith embraces at once all the attributes of God; therefore, faith has confidence in God and does not seek to understand everything before yielding the heart to Him. There are, and must be, multitudes of things that we cannot understand, nor would it be useful for us to understand at present.

Faith overcomes the obstacles to belief.

We see how faith disposes of these difficulties. Since God's attributes are what He declares them to be, there are things that cannot be explained to finite beings. For example, take the doctrine of the Trinity. Human reason cannot explain the Trinity, nor is any explanation called for; God simply announces the fact in the Bible, that the Father, the Son, and the Spirit are God. We find that at one time, before the destruction of Sodom, three individuals appeared to Abraham, and one of them who is called Jehovah, informed Abraham what they were going to do, and Abraham put up a prayer to have Sodom saved—you recollect the afflicting circumstance. We learn that there were three men, or apparently so; two of them probably were angels in human form, and the other was no less a being than Jehovah himself. Now take note of this! Who can doubt but that God could have assumed the same form in millions of cases at the same time in different parts of the world, for there would be nothing contrary to reason in that. There is nothing then unreasonable in the supposition that God should exist in three persons or three hundred thousand million persons! We say there is nothing unreasonable in it. Who does not know that there is not? What then do people mean when they say that they cannot believe in the Trinity? Why not believe in the Trinity? What do such people suppose they know about infinity? Can they affirm of the Father, Son, and Holy Spirit that these three cannot exercise and manifest the attributes of God? But, as God announced the fact there does not need to be any evidence of it to the person who has faith. Faith makes no effort to understand it. If you object to this, let me ask, "How do you know that you exist yourself?" O yes, you say, we know that we exist; we believe it. What makes you believe it? Can you explain it? Did you choose your body? Can you tell the connection between matter and spirit? How can you prove what you are?

Some years ago, I was walking with a gentleman in the city of New

99

York. We were talking about religion and mind, and he stopped right in the street, and said, "You say such and such things about mind; now what is mind?" "If you tell me," said I, "what matter is, I will tell you what mind is." "Why," said he, "matter has the property of extension, solidity, and so forth;" but he did not name any of the primary attributes of matter. "Well," I replied "mind wills, thinks, feels, and the like." He looked at me quite astonished. I continued, "You have told me some of the attributes of matter, can you tell what those attributes are?" "I do not know," said he. "Neither can I explain what the substance of mind is." If the wisest philosopher in the universe were standing in this pulpit, a little child might ask him such questions as he could not answer or explain, any more than we can explain the doctrine of the Trinity—not a bit. There is not a single thing in the universe in all the kingdom of nature, when you come to dive to the bottom of it, which is not as difficult to explain as any doctrine of the Bible. Why believe in any of these things? Why believe in your own existence? The fact is that people do not disbelieve things because they are mysterious until they come to the subject of religion, because the world around them is so deeply mysterious, that there is not a single thing that they can understand to the bottom, yet they believe in them. It is very frequently the case that people do not realize that there is a mystery in anything but religion.

Now I know that philosophy can in part explain many things, and that those things which a few years ago were considered mysterious, and even marvelous, are now understood. Science has already placed the human race in a position to explain the theory of many things that were deep mysteries, and spread them out before the minds of people. But, speaking generally, both with regard to the spiritual and the natural world, people must live by faith. They believe in the various things around them in the natural world although they may not be able to understand them. The same is true of spiritual things. We must receive much on testimony that cannot be explained to us. Probably, in many cases, God would not explain them to us even if we could understand them, because it would not be well for us, but God leads us step by step to a correct understanding of things that may be useful and necessary for us to know.

In relation to the question of sin, and its necessary attendant misery as it exists in our world, there is a mystery about it. Of course, every mind affirms that where sin is, there misery ought to be. But the questions of wonder are how sin came into the world and why it was permitted? That this is a wise order of things no one can doubt. God made humans superior to all the rest of the inhabitants of this globe. We see by the power, sagacity, and knowledge of human beings that God designed them to be the head of creation. But take note of this! Human beings are in rebellion against God. This is a simple matter of fact. There is nothing more certain in the universe than that human beings as a race have set God at naught and bid Him defiance. Now reason affirms that the curse of God should be written upon everything in the universe in order to testify to God's real character; that God's character should not be mistaken. But while we see that God does testify against sin, there are also indications that He has a strong disposition to be merciful as far as He wisely can; but the difficulties are many, and great, in the way of His forgiving sin.

Faith in God does not find it very difficult to remove all these obstructions. Disbelief says, sin exists. When looking at God's government, as a system of moral law, it does not appear that sin can be forgiven. In such a government, disbelief says, pardon is impossible. But faith says at once, God is kind, wise, and good, as well as infinitely powerful. Misery and sin exist, but they are allowed to continue in the world only for a wise purpose, to assist in bringing about the end at which God aims. For although sin is a great abomination, God will bring good out of it. Look at the sin of Judas. The devil put it into his heart to betray the Son of God to His enemies. To his dismay, he saw the greatness of his crime; but God overruled their evil intentions. His purpose was that the blood of His dear Son should be shed as an atonement for sin.

Although we cannot understand the reason why God should permit the existence of sin in the world at all, faith can easily dispose of the difficulties which may suggest themselves. Faith believes that everything that God does must be infinitely good and wise. The fact is, unbelief in such matters is the most unreasonable thing in the world. If you profess not to believe anything until you understand it, why do you believe in your own existence? What do you know of volition? You move your muscles, but you cannot understand exactly how. Faith disposes of all these difficul-

7

Romans 4:20-21

ties and is reasonable when so doing. Take Abraham's case. God promises that Abraham shall have a son. "I shall have it," he says, "I am very old, and Sarah is very old; no matter how old, God is able to give us a son." The child is born and growing up when God calls to Abraham and tells him to go and offer Isaac as a sacrifice. Abraham says, "I will go. God has a good reason for the requirement. I know He must. He cannot have any other. He is infinitely good and infinitely wise. He cannot have made any mistake. The path of duty is plain. I will walk in it." "O," asks unbelief, "How will the promise be fulfilled, 'In Isaac shall thy seed be called?'" "I do not know," says Abraham, "but God is able to raise him from the dead." Thus, you see his faith very quickly disposed of the difficulty although it was very great. Now is there anything inconsistent with reason in all this? No. Just look at it right in the face.

My own reason tells me that God is infinitely perfect in all His attributes, everywhere and in everything, and that either permissively or actively God is concerned in everything that takes place. I find myself in a universe surrounded by a multitude of things that I cannot explain, and that even God himself could not explain to me because of my limited capacity, but these things are true. As the law of progression operates, I come to understand many things that were before dark and inexplicable to my mind. Reason tells us there must be many things in the government of an infinite God that a finite mind cannot comprehend. When a person is in a spiritual state of mind, faith takes the place of knowledge. The little child, for instance, lives by faith. Human society exists by faith. Destroy all confidence, all faith, and society could not exist and no business could be transacted. In the spiritual state of human beings, faith is just as necessary

God has a design in view with regard to these trials of our faith. Everyone can see that one great object is to strengthen faith. I have often heard it remarked, by intelligent people too, that in heaven faith would not exist because there we shall walk by sight. Now there is some truth in that, but much greater error. It is true that many things that we merely believe here, we shall know there. Still, there will be much to call forth our faith in heaven. There must be in the government of God much that it would require millions of ages to understand, and we shall go on acquiring knowledge throughout the immensity of eternity; thus, there will be need of faith in God in eternity as in time; it will be as true in heaven as on earth. Suppose the angels did not have faith: the fall of Adam must have given a shock to the inhabitants of heaven. However, they believed that God had some wise design when He permitted Adam to fall. Faith disposes of everything this way: let what will, come; there is no alarm or doubt but that all will be right.

I had intended to show that those who stumble and stagger must lose the blessing consequent upon believing, as a natural necessity, which every one can see must be the case, but I see that I must close with one remark.

REMARKS

There is no hope for those who will not believe God. Suppose you had a family of children and they should lose confidence in you as a businessman. They would stagger and stumble at every step you took, just because you could not explain to them all your plans. You say to them, "Dear children, I cannot explain these things to you. I am laboring for your good; therefore, be quiet, passive, and have confidence in me that all will be well." However, if they will not, what can you do with them? They must remain in their unbelieving, unconverted state. Now, it is the same in God's government. There are many things that cannot be explained to human beings; so, some will not exercise faith, and if they persist in their unbelief, they will go stumbling and fretting to the gates of hell! Some people will take nothing on trust. They must catechize their Maker. If God does not explain everything to them, they have no confidence in Him. Hence, it is said that they shall have their part with liars in the lake of fire. My dear hearers, the most unreasonable and blasphemous abomination in the world is unbelief.

7

Romans 4:20-21

---

* Charles G. Finney, "The Penny Pulpit," preached on Sunday morning, January 12, 1851, at The Tabernacle, Moorfields, England, *Principles of Faith*, 23–31. For Review: Answer the Study Questions on page 178, Cowles page 199.

The Psalms on Righteousness

He will make your righteousness shine like the dawn, the justice of your cause like the noonday sun. —Psalm 37:6

I proclaim righteousness in the great assembly; I do not seal my lips, as you know, O LORD. I do not hide your righteousness in my heart; I speak of your faithfulness and salvation. I do not conceal your love and your truth from the great assembly. —Psalm 40:9-10

You love righteousness and hate wickedness; therefore God, your God, has set you above your companions by anointing you with the oil of joy. —Psalm 45:7

You answer us with awesome deeds of righteousness, O God our Savior, the hope of all the ends of the earth and of the farthest seas. —Psalm 65:5

I will come and proclaim your mighty acts, O Sovereign LORD; I will proclaim your righteousness, yours alone. —Psalm 71:16

Your righteousness reaches to the skies, O God, you who have done great things. Who, O God, is like you? —Psalm 71:19

Love and faithfulness meet together; righteousness and peace kiss each other. Faithfulness springs forth from the earth, and righteousness looks down from heaven. The LORD will indeed give what is good, and our land will yield its harvest. Righteousness goes before him and prepares the way for his steps. —Psalm 85:10-13

They rejoice in your name all day long; they exult in your righteousness. —Psalm 89:16 (More on page 114)

8

God's Love Commended to Us
1858

God commendeth his love toward us, in that, while we were yet sinners, Christ died for us. —Romans 5:8—KJV

God demonstrates his own love for us in this: While we were still sinners, Christ died for us. —Romans 5:8—NIV

What does Saint Paul mean by "commend"? He means to "recommend:" to set forth in a clear and strong light. Toward whom does God exercise His love? Toward us: toward our lost race. He manifests His love to every person: "For God so loved the world, that he gave his only begotten Son, that whosoever believeth in him should not perish, but have everlasting life" (John 3:16—KJV).

How does He commend His love? By giving His Son to die for us. By giving one who was a Son and a Son well-beloved. The Bible says that Christ Jesus "gave himself a ransom for all" (1 Timothy 2:6), "that he by the grace of God should taste death for every man" (Hebrews 2:9). We are not to suppose that He died for the sum total of mankind in such a sense that His death is not truly for each one in particular. It is a great mistake into which some fall, to suppose that Christ died for the race in general, and not for each one in particular. By this mistake, the gospel is likely to lose much of its practical power on our hearts. We need to apprehend it as Paul did, who said of Jesus Christ that He "loved me, and gave himself for me" (Gal 2:20). We need to make this personal application of Christ's death. No doubt this was the great secret of Paul's holy life, and of his great power in preaching the gospel. We need to regard Jesus as having loved us personally and individually. Let us consider how much pains God has taken to make us feel that He cares for us personally. It is so in His providence and in His gospel. He would gladly make us single ourselves from the mass and feel that His loving eye and heart are upon us individually.

Why does God commend His love to us?

For what end does He commend His love to us? Is it an ambition to make a display? Surely, there can be no affectation in His recommending His love to us. God is infinitely above all artificiality. He must from His very nature act honestly. Of course, He must have some good reason for this manifestation of His love. No doubt, He seeks to prove to us the reality of His love. Feeling the most perfect love toward our lost race, He deemed it best to reveal this love and make it manifest, both to us and to all His creatures. What could evince His love, if this gift of His Son does not? O, how gloriously is love revealed in this great sacrifice of God's Son! How this makes divine love stand out prominently before the universe! What else could He have done that would prove His love so effectually?

God would show that His love is unselfish, for Jesus did not die for us as His friends, but as His enemies. It was while we were yet sinners and enemies of God that Christ died for us. On this point, Paul suggests that "scarcely for a righteous man will one die; yet peradventure for a good man, some would even dare to die" (Romans 5:7—KJV) But the human race was as far as possible from being good. Indeed, we were not even righteous, but were utterly wicked. For a very dear friend one might be willing to die. There have been soldiers who, to save the life of a beloved officer, have taken into their own bosom the shaft of death; however, for one who was merely just and not so much as good, this sacrifice could scarcely be made. How much less for an enemy! Herein we may see how greatly "God commendeth His love to us, in that while we were yet sinners (enemies of God), Christ died for us" (Romans 5:8—KJV). Notice yet further; this love of God to us cannot be the love of esteem or complacency, because there is in us no ground for such a love. It can be no other than the love of unselfish benevolence. Satan called in question this love in Eden. He made bold to insinuate, "Hath your God indeed said, Ye shall not eat of every tree in the garden?" (Genesis 3:1—KJV). Satan implied, "Why should God wish to debar you from such a pleasure?" The old Serpent sought to cast suspicion on the benevolence of God. Hence, there was the more reason why God should vindicate His love.

He would also commend the great strength of His love. We should think we gave evidence of strong love, if we were to give our friend a great sum of money. But what is any sum of money compared with giving up a dear Son to die? O, surely, it is surpassing love, beyond measure wonderful, that Jesus should not only labor and suffer, but should really die! Was ever love like this?

God designed to reveal the moral character of His love for people, and especially the justice of His love. He could not show favors to the guilty until He made His government secure and duly honored His law. Without the sacrifice of His Son, He knew it would not be safe to pardon sinners. God must maintain the honor of His throne. He must show that He could never "wink at" or ignore sin. He felt the solemn necessity of giving a public rebuke of sin before the universe. This rebuke was the more expressive because Jesus Christ himself was sinless. Of course, in the death of Jesus Christ, God was not frowning on His sin (for He was without sin), but on the sin of those whose sins He bore and in whose place He stood.

This shows God's abhorrence of sin since Jesus stood as our representative. While He stood in this position, God could not spare Him, but laid on Him the chastisement of our iniquities. O, what a rebuke of sin

8

Romans 5:8

was that! How expressively did it show that God abhorred sin, yet loved the sinner! These were among the great objects in view—to beget in our souls the two-fold conviction of His love for us and of our abhorrent sin against Him. He would make those convictions strong and abiding; therefore, He sets forth Jesus crucified before our eyes—a far more expressive thing than any mere words. No saying that He loved us could approximate toward the strength and impressiveness of this manifestation. In no other way could He make it seem so much a reality—so touching and so overpowering. Thus, He commends it to our regard. Thus, He invites us to look at it. He tells us that the angels desire to look into it. He would have us weigh this great fact and examine all its bearings until it shall come full upon our souls with its power to save. He commends His love to us that we might reciprocate His love, as if He would incite us to love Him Who has so loved us. Of course, He would have us understand this love, and appreciate it, that we may requite it with responsive love in return. It is an example for us that we may love our enemies and, much more, our brothers and sisters in Christ. O, when this love has taken its effect on our hearts, how deeply do we feel that we cannot hate any one for whom Christ died! Then instead of selfishly thrusting our neighbor off, and grasping the good to which his claim is fully as great as ours is, we love him with a love so deep and so pure that it cannot be in our heart to do him wrong.

It was thus a part of the divine purpose to show us what true love is. As one said in prayer, "We thank Thee, Father, that Thou hast given us Thy Son to teach us how to love." Yes, God would let us know that He himself is love, and hence that if we would be His children, we too must love Him and love one another. He would reveal His love to draw us into sympathy with himself and make us like Him. Do you not suppose that a thorough consideration of God's love, as manifested in Christ, does actually teach us what love is, and serve to draw our souls into such love? The question is often asked, "How shall I love?" This example gives the answer. Herein is love! Look at it and drink in its spirit. People are prone to love themselves supremely. Here is a totally different sort of love from that. God's love commends itself in that while we were yet sinners, Christ died for us. How forcibly does this rebuke our selfishness! How much we need this lesson to subdue our narrow selfishness, our self-centeredness, our shame, and our unbelief!

How strange it is that people do not realize the love of God! The wife of a minister, who had herself labored in many revivals, said to me, "I never, until a few days ago, knew that God is love." "What do you mean?" I asked. "I mean that I never apprehended it in all its bearings before." O, I assure you, it is a great and blessed truth, and it is a great thing to see it as it is! When God's love becomes a reality to the soul, and you come under its powerful sympathy, then you will find the gospel indeed the power of God unto salvation. Paul prayed for his Ephesian converts that they might "be able to comprehend with all saints what is the breadth and length and depth and height; and to know the love of God that passeth knowledge, that they might be filled with all the fullness of God" (Ephesians 3:18, 19—KJV).

God sought, in thus commending His love to us, to subdue our slavish fear. Someone said, "When I was young, I was sensible of fearing God, but I knew I did not love Him. The instruction I received led me to fear, but not to love." So long as we think of God only as One to be feared, not to be loved, there will be a prejudice against Him as more an enemy than a friend. Every sinner knows that he deserves God's hatred. He sees plainly that God must have good reasons to be displeased with him. The selfish sinner judges God from the viewpoint of himself. Knowing how he feels toward those who wrong him, he unconsciously infers that God must feel so toward every sinner. When he tries to pray, his heart will not go out to God, for he feels nothing but terror. He feels no attraction toward God, no real love. The childlike spirit comes before God, weeping indeed, but also loving and trusting. Now the state of feeling which fears only, God would happily put away, and make us know that He loves us still. We must not regard Him as being altogether such as ourselves. He would undeceive us and make us realize that though He has "spoken against us, yet He does earnestly remember us still" (Jeremiah 31:20—KJV). He would have us interpret His dealings fairly and without prejudice. He sees how, when He thwarts people's plans, that they are bent on misunderstanding Him. They will think that He is reckless of their welfare, and they are blind to the precious truth that He shapes all His ways toward them in love and kindness. He would lead us to judge thus, that if God spared not His own Son, but gave Him up freely for us all, then He will much more give us all things else most freely.

God would lead us to serve Him in love and not in bondage. He would draw us forth into the liberty of the sons of God. He loves to see the obedience of the heart. He would inspire love enough to make all our service free, cheerful, and full of joy. If you wish to make others love you, you must give them your love. Show your servants the love of your heart, so will you break their bondage and make their service one of love. In this way, God commends His love toward us in order to win our hearts to himself, and thus get us ready and fit to dwell forever in His eternal home. His ultimate aim is to save us from our sins that He may fill us forever with His own joy and peace.

REMARKS

We see that saving faith must be the heart's belief of this great fact that God so loved us. Saving faith receives the death of Christ as an expression of God's love to us. No other sort of faith—no faith in anything else—wins our heart to love God. Saving faith saves us from our bondage and our prejudice against Him. It is this which makes it saving. Any faith that leaves out this great truth must fail to save us. If any one element of faith is vital, it is this. If anyone doubts this fact of God's love in Christ, I would not give much for all his religion. It is worthless.

The Old Testament system is full of teaching about God's love. All those bloody sacrifices are full of it. When the priest, in behalf of all the people, came forward and laid his hand on the head of the innocent victim, and then confessed his sins and the sins of all, and then when this animal was slain and its blood poured out before the Lord, and He gave tokens that He accepted the offering, it was a solemn manifestation that God substituted for the sufferings due the sinner, the death of an innocent lamb. Throughout that ancient system, we find the same idea, showing how God would have people see His love in the gift of His own dear Son.

One great reason people find it so difficult to repent and submit to God is they do not receive this great fact—do not accept it in simple faith. If they were to accept it and let it come home to their hearts, it would carry with it a power to subdue their hearts to submission and to love.

One reason young people are so afraid they may receive a call to the ministry is their lack of confidence in the love of God. O, if they saw and believed in His great love, surely they would not let eight hundred millions go down to hell in ignorance of this gospel! O, how it would agonize their heart that so many should go to their graves and to an eternal hell, and never know the love of Jesus to their perishing souls! Yet here is a young man for whom Christ has died, who cannot bear to go and tell them they have a Savior! What do you think of his magnanimity? How much is his heart like Christ's heart? Do you wonder that Paul could not hold his peace, but felt that he must go to the ends of the earth and preach the name of Jesus where it had never been known before? How deeply he felt that he must let the world know these glad tidings of great joy! How amazing that young people now can let the gospel die unknown and not go forth to bless the lost! Ah, did they ever taste its blessedness? Have they ever known its power? Do you solemnly intend to conceal it, that it may never bless your dying brethren?

This matter of commending God's love is the strongest and most expressive He could employ. In no other way possible could He so forcibly demonstrate His great love to our human race. Hence, if this fails to subdue people's enmity, prejudice, and unbelief, what can avail? What methods shall He use if this proves unavailing to them? The Bible demands, "How shall we escape, if we neglect so great salvation?" (Hebrews 2:3—KJV). Well may it make this appeal, for if this fails to win us, what can succeed?

If we had been His friends, there would have been no need of His dying for us. It was only because we were yet sinners that He died for us. How great, then, are the claims of this love on our hearts!

Sinners often think that if they were pious and good, the Lord might love them. Therefore, they try to win His love by doing some good things. They try in every such way to make God love them, and especially by mending their manners rather than their hearts. Alas, they seem not to know that the very fact of their being sunk so low in sin is moving God's

8

Romans 5:8

heart to its very foundations! A sinless angel enjoys God's complacency, but not His pity; he is not an object of pity, and there is no call for it. The same is true of a good child. He receives the complacency of his parents, but not their compassion. However, suppose this child becomes vicious. Then his parents mourn over his fall, and their compassion is moved. They look on him with pity and anxiety as they see him going down to the depths of vice, crime, and degradation. More and more as he sinks lower and lower in the filth and abominations of sin, they mourn over him; and as they see how changed he is, they stand in tears, saying, "Alas, this is our son, our once-honored son! But how fallen now! Our heart is moved for him, and there is nothing we would not do or suffer, if we might save him!" Likewise, the sinner's great degradation moves the compassions of his divine Father to their very depths. When the Lord passes by and sees him lying in his blood in the open field, He says that is my son! He bears the image of his Maker. "Since I have spoken against him, I do earnestly remember him still; therefore my bowels are troubled for him: I will surely have mercy upon him, saith the Lord" (Jeremiah 31:20—KJV). Sinners should remember that the very fact of their being sinners is the thing that moves God's compassion and pity. Do you ask, "I do not see how God can make it consistent with His holiness to pardon and love such a sinner as I am?" I can tell you how: "By giving His own Son to die in your place!"

Christ died for us that He might save us, and save us from our sins. Must it not grieve Him exceedingly if we continue in sin? What do you think? Suppose you were to see Jesus face to face, and He were to show you those wounds in His hands and in His side, and were to say, "I died for you because I saw you lost beyond hope, and because I would save you from your sins; and now, will you repeat those sins again? Can you go on yet longer to sin against me?"

You may infer from our subject that Jesus must be willing to save you from wrath, if you truly repent and accept Him as your Savior. How can you doubt it? Having suffered unto death for this very purpose, surely, it only remains for you to meet the conditions for Him to save you from wrath.

You may infer also that God, having spared not His Son, will also with

Him freely give you all things else: grace enough to meet all your needs; the kind care of His providence; the love of His heart; everything you can need. To continue in sin in spite of such grace and love must be monstrous! It must grieve His heart exceedingly.

A friend of mine who has charge of one hundred and fifty boys in a Reform School is accustomed, when they misbehave, to put them for a time on bread and water. What do you think he does himself in some of these cases? He goes and puts himself with them on bread and water! The boys in the school see this, and they learn love of their superintendent and father. Now, when tempted to crime, they must say to themselves, "If I do wrong, I shall have to live on bread and water; but the worst of all is, my father will come and eat bread and water with me and for my sake; and how can I bear that? How can I bear to have my father who loves me so well, confine himself to bread and water for my sake!"

So Jesus puts himself in pain and shame and death that you might have joy and life, that you might be forgiven and saved from sinning; and now will you go on to sin more? Have you no heart to appreciate His dying love? Can you go on and sin yet more and none the less for all the love shown you on Calvary?

You understand that Christ died to redeem you from sin. Suppose your own eyes were to see Him face to face, and He should tell you all He has done for you. "Sister," He says, "I died to save you from that sin; will you do it again? Can you go on and sin just the same as if I had never died for you?"

In that Reform School of which I spoke, the effects produced on even the worst boys by the love shown them is really striking. The Superintendent had long insisted that he did not want locks and bars to confine his boys. The Directors had said, "You must lock them in; if you don't they will run away." On one occasion, the Superintendent was to be absent two weeks. A Director came to him urging that he must lock up the boys before he left, for while he was absent, they would certainly run away. The Superintendent replied, "I think not. I have confidence in those boys." "But," replied the Director, "give us some guarantee. Are you willing to pledge your city lot on the condition that if they do run away the lot will go into the Reform School Fund?" After a little reflection, he consented, and replied, "I will give you my lot and all the little property I have in the world if any of my boys run away while I am gone." Before he set off, he called all the boys together. He explained to them his pledge and asked them to look at his dependent family, and then appealed to their honor and their love for him. "Would you be willing to see me stripped of all my property? I think I can trust you." He went and returned a little unexpectedly and late on one Saturday night. Scarcely had he entered the yard, when the word rang through the sleeping halls, "Our father has come!" And almost in a moment they were there greeting him and shouting, "We are all here! We are all here!"

Cannot Christ's love have as much power as that? Shall the love the Reform School boys bear to their official father hold them to their place during the long days and nights of his absence; and shall not Christ's love to us restrain us from sinning? What do you say? Will you say thus? "If Christ loves me so much, then it is plain He won't send me to hell, and therefore I will go on and sin all I please." Do you say that? Then there is no hope for you. The gospel that ought to save you can do nothing for you but sink you deeper in moral and eternal ruin. If you say this, then you are fully committed to pervert the gospel to your utter damnation! If those Reform School boys had said, "Our Father loves us so well, he will eat bread and water with us, and therefore we know he will not punish us to hurt us;" would they not certainly bring a curse on themselves? Would not their reformation be utterly hopeless? Therefore, of the sinner who can make light of the Savior's dying love. O, is it possible that when Jesus has died for you to save your soul from sin and from hell that you can sin again and yet again? Will you live on in sin only the more, because He has loved you so much? Think of this and make up your mind. Say: "If Christ has died to redeem me from sin, then away with all sinning henceforth and forever. I forsake all my sins from this hour! I can afford to live or to die with my Redeemer. So help me God. I will have no more to do with sinning forever!"*

---

* Charles G. Finney, "The Oberlin Evangelist," July 21, 1858, as "God's Love to Us," *Sermons on Gospel Themes*, 307–318, *Principles of Victory*, 55–62. For Review: Answer the Study Questions on page 179, Cowles page 200.

9

The Nature of Death to Sin
1840

For he that is dead is freed from sin. —Romans 6:7—KJV

Because anyone who has died has been freed from sin. —Romans 6:7—NIV

In discussing death to sin, I intend to notice the different kinds of death mentioned in the Bible and then look closely at what Paul means by death in our text. I will discuss what death to sin consists in, what death to sin implies, and how we can live in a state of death to sin.

The different kinds of death.

In the Bible, we learn about natural death, which is the death of the body. We also learn about spiritual death, which is death in sin. Spiritual death is total depravity or a state of entire alienation from God. Eternal death is the endless curse of God.

In Romans 6, Paul wrote of death to sin. This is very evident from the context. At the close of the preceding chapter, Paul spoke of the super-abounding grace of Christ. Then he commenced the sixth chapter by saying, "What shall we say then? Shall we continue in sin, that grace may abound? God forbid. How shall we that are dead to sin live any longer therein?" (Romans 6:1, 2—KJV). Here Paul is speaking of those who were alive and yet dead to sin. He spoke of their having received a baptism into the death of Christ. By their spiritual baptism, they solemnly set themselves apart or consecrated themselves to the death of Christ: "Know ye not, that so many of us as were baptized into Jesus Christ were baptized into his death? Therefore we are buried with him by baptism into death; that like as Christ was raised up from the dead by the glory of the Father, even so we also should walk in newness of life. For if we have been planted together in the likeness of his death, we shall be also in the likeness of his resurrection; knowing this, that our old man is crucified with Him, that the body of sin might be destroyed, that henceforth we should not serve sin. For he that is dead is freed from sin. Now, if we be dead with Christ, we believe that we shall also live with him" (Romans 6:3-8—KJV). Paul speaks of them as not only dead, but also by their spiritual baptism buried into the death of Christ. To carry the idea of their being still further from the life of sin, He speaks of them as being planted into the likeness of His death, and crucified with Him that the body of sin might be destroyed. Then Paul adds in the words of the text, "Now he that is dead is freed from sin." In the margin of my Bible, the text reads "is justified from sin." The term here rendered justification may be rendered "is made righteous." It is plain from this connection that Paul is speaking of those who had been so baptized by the Holy Spirit so as to be dead to sin, buried, planted, crucified, as it respects sin.

What is death to sin and death in sin?

Death to sin consists in the annihilation of selfishness, and the reign of perfect love to God and man in the heart and life.

Death to sin is the opposite of death in sin. Death in sin implies living for self, or being dead to God's glory and interests and only alive to our own glory. Death to sin implies the reverse of this. It implies a death to our own interests and happiness as an end of pursuit, and a living wholly to the glory of God, and for the up building of His kingdom.

Death in sin implies a will opposed to the will of God. I speak here of a fixed and permanent state of the will in opposition to a single particular volition. A will in this state labeled "death in sin" is not at all influenced by the will of God. It has never submitted to God's will, and consequently a knowledge of the will of God is no influential reason to determine its volitions. However, death to sin implies a will wholly subservient to and under the control of the will of God.

I speak of *a state* of will. One who is dead to sin has no other will than that God's will should in all things be done. Lay before him any question in which he is in doubt in respect to what the will of God is, and he will find himself unable to decide upon a course of action. All he can decide upon in such a case is to search and inquire what is the will of God. Until he is satisfied in some way in respect to the will of God, he is utterly in doubt and finds himself unable to make up his mind and come to any decision with respect to the question before him. This is a state of mind directly opposite to a state of mind called "death in sin." In a state of death in sin, the will of God is not inquired after as the great and only influential motive to decide the will. A man in this state has, as we say, a will of his own. He decides upon his own responsibility, in his own strength, and entirely in view of his own selfish reasons. A person who is dead to sin has so submitted himself to the will of God—so bowed his will to God's will—that he decides nothing in view of selfish reasons; the will of God has come to be the controlling reason or motive of his conduct. Let him but know what is the will of God in the case, and his will is yielding as air. However, shut him out from this knowledge, and he is in a state of the utmost perplexity and cannot decide upon any course of conduct. He can only say, I have no will about it.

However uncommon it has been for Christians to come into this state while in life and health, it has not been at all uncommon for them to be in this state while on their deathbed. Everyone conversant with deathbed scenes has probably witnessed such cases of entire surrender of the whole being to the will of God, as that the individual was unable to choose whether to live or die and could only say, "I have no will about it." Not

9

Romans 6:7

knowing what the will of God was, there was no other choice than this, that the will of God, whatever it was, should be done. Ask an individual whether sick or well, living or dying, who is in this state, whether he wills or chooses a certain thing. If it be a question in respect to which he is in doubt as to what the will of God is, you will find him to be entirely at a loss. He is conscious of choosing that the will of God should be done. But until he knows whether this or that is the will of God he has no choice about that particular event.

Death in sin implies a self-indulgent state of mind. To consult ones own ease, happiness, reputation, and interests is natural to him who is dead in sin. If he is on board a steamboat, you will find him ready to contend for the best berth, and hastening to obtain the best seat at the first table. If riding in a stagecoach you will observe him seeking for the best seat. To consult his own comfort, his own indulgence and happiness is the law of his mind. And in ten thousand ways will this state of mind develop itself. However, a death to sin implies a self-denying state of mind, a disposition to give others the preference, a choosing to accommodate others, and bless, and benefit others at the expense of self-interest or self-indulgence.

A death in sin implies the real and practical regarding of ourselves as our own. But death to sin is the real and practical regarding of our whole being as God's.

A death in sin implies the love of our own reputation. Death to sin implies the making of ourselves no reputation as Christ did.

A death in sin implies the practical regarding of our possessions as our own. Death to sin implies the real and practical regarding of our possessions as God's.

Death in sin implies the dominion of the flesh and a will in subjection to the flesh. A death to sin implies a subjection of the body to the soul. A death to sin implies keeping the body under and bringing it into subjection so all its appetites and propensities are brought into subjection to the will of God.

A death in sin implies a state of mind that is influenced by sensible objects, by the honors, riches, opinions, and things of this world as much as if its possessor expected to live here forever. Death to sin implies the giving up the world substantially as a dying man gives it up. Its riches, honors, amusements, pursuits, ambition, strifes, and envyings, what are all these to him? If he knows himself to be a dying man, he regards them not. He desires them not. He seeks them not. He does not, cannot, under these circumstances, will to have them. He chooses nothing of this world's goods, but those things that are really necessary for the few hours or moments which remain to him of this life. A little more breath—perhaps a few spoons full of water—a little of the kind attention of his friends are all that is left for him to desire of earthly good. Now death to sin implies this giving up of all desire and expectation of the wealth, honors, and selfish pursuits of this world. The man who is dead to sin is as absolutely satisfied with a competency of earthly good as a man is who is on a bed of death. He would no sooner lay his schemes of earthly aggrandizement, or for enlarging and perpetuating his selfish gratification, than a man would upon a bed of death. In a word, he has given up the world as an object of pursuit, as really and emphatically as if he knew himself to be doomed to live but one hour. He has entered upon a new and eternal life. All his plans, desires, and aims are heavenly, and not earthly, sensual or devilish.

How to enter into and exercise this state of mind, which is "death to sin".

You cannot experience "death to sin" as a state of mind by the strength of your own resolutions. You will never die to sin by merely resolving to die to sin. It is one of the most common delusions to suppose that you can stand against temptation by the strength of your own resolutions. Peter thought himself able to follow Christ even unto death. But his resolution, like all mere human resolutions, failed him just when he most needed its support. A Christian brother said to me the other day, "I have learned this about my resolutions; they are firm enough when there is nothing to overthrow them and I do not need their support. But they always fail me when I do. Just when I have a trial that demands their sustaining power, I find they are like air and good for nothing."

This state of mind is never to be entered into by any unaided efforts of our own. Sin has too long had dominion over us. Our powers are too much enslaved by the protracted indulgence of sin. Sin has too long been our master to be at once put down by any unaided efforts of ours.

This state of mind is effected by the baptism of the Holy Spirit. The baptism of the Spirit does not imply the bestowment of miraculous gifts, as some seem to have supposed. The Apostles possessed miraculous gifts before they were baptized with the Holy Spirit. The power of miracles may or may not be incidental to spiritual baptism. Miracles, by no means, constitute any part of it. Nor does spiritual baptism imply great excitement.

The baptism of the Holy Spirit does imply such a degree of divine influence as will purify the heart. The New Testament writers manifestly use the term baptism as synonymous with purifying. Water baptism is typical of spiritual baptism. Spiritual baptism is the purifying of the heart by the Holy Spirit. Miraculous gifts, great excitement of mind, great rejoicings, or great sorrowing over sin, may be incidental to spiritual baptism, but they are not essential to it. Those who have read the memoir of J. B. Taylor will recollect that on April 23, 1822, while he was engaged in prayer, he felt his whole soul sweetly yielding itself up to God.* Such a sweet thorough yielding himself and all his interests for time and eternity into the hands of God he had never before experienced. Now I suppose that this was the effect of the baptism of the Holy Spirit. He ever after remained in a state of mind entirely different from anything he had before experienced.

In receiving the baptism of the Holy Spirit we are by no means passive but eminently active. We secure the influence of the Holy Spirit by faith. Faith in Christ throws the mind open to the influence of His truth and gives the Spirit the opportunity of so presenting truth as sweetly to bring the entire person under its whole power. Christ administers spiritual blessings, and this is received by taking hold of His promise to baptize with the Holy Spirit and throwing your mind open to His influences.

The baptism of the Apostles by the Holy Spirit on the day of Pentecost will illustrate what I mean. Christ had promised them that they should be baptized with the Holy Spirit not many days hence. They fastened upon His promise and waited in a constant attitude of prayer and expectation. They threw the door of their minds open to His influence. Now Christ has given to all believers a great many promises of the freeness of the Holy Spirit. He has said that the "Father is more willing to give the Holy Spirit to them that ask him than earthly parents are to give good gifts to their children" (Luke 11:13—KJV). The "water of life" which is so abundantly promised in both the New and Old Testaments is the Holy Spirit. This everyone knows who has attentively considered the real meaning of those promises.

If you would enter into this death to sin, you must be baptized with the Holy Spirit. If you would be baptized with the Holy Spirit, you must fasten upon the promises of Christ and take hold of them in faith, laying your whole soul open to receive His influences. Rest with the utmost confidence in His promise to give you of the "fountain of water of life freely" (see Revelation 21:6; 22:1, 17). When you have taken hold of His promise, be sure not to let go or let your confidence be shaken until you feel a consciousness that "you are baptized into his death" (Romans 6:3).

REMARKS

In the connection of this text, Paul speaks of himself and others as dead to and freed from sin. If death to sin does not imply entire sanctification, death in sin does not imply total depravity, for they are manifestly opposite states of mind. As death in sin is consistent with persons doing many things which the world regards as righteous, so death to sin may be consistent with many things which the world would regard as sinful.

Paul's history confirms the profession which he here makes of being dead to sin. The circumstances of the primitive Church rendered a death to sin almost inevitable, at least in many instances. The profession of attachment to Christ must inevitably cost many of them all that the world holds or calls dear. They had to enter upon the Christian life by a renunciation of the world, by giving up worldly expectations and pursuits, as much as people do on a bed of death. This state of public sentiment was eminently calculated to facilitate their entrance into a state of spiritual death, and was no doubt a prime reason for their rapid advancement in the divine life.

We see why it is that state and other violent persecutions have already greatly contributed to the spirituality of the Church. We see also why it

9

Romans 6:7

is that state and worldly favor has crippled the energies and overthrown the purity of the Church. We see how the idea comes to be so prevalent that Christians are not wholly sanctified until death. As a matter of fact, this no doubt generally is true, that Christians are not wholly and permanently sanctified until about the close of life, until they come into that state in which they expect very soon to die. I once knew a good man who was told by his physicians that in consequence of the enlargement of the large blood vessel near the heart he was exposed to instant death, and that at all events he must expect to die very soon. This news, after the first shock was over, was instrumental in baptizing him into the death of Christ. He very soon entered into a most blessed and heavenly state of mind, let go of the world, and seemed to stand looking and waiting with most heavenly serenity for the coming of the Son of Man. In this state of mind, his doctors told him that he might probably live for a long time notwithstanding his disease. This so staggered him as to well nigh bring him again into bondage. Not seeming to understand the philosophy of the state of mind in which he was, and how to remain in it by simple faith, he staggered and groaned under this intelligence until Christ, true to His promise, interposed and set his feet upon the eternal rock. After this he lived and died to the wonder of all those around him, few if any of whom perhaps so much as dreamed that his state of mind was what is intended by a "death to sin."

Edward Payson** and multitudes of good people have found it easy to enter into this state of mind when they relinquished all expectation of remaining longer in this world. It seems impossible or difficult for most people to conceive that this state of mind may be really entered into with a prospect of any amount of life still before us. However, there is no need of waiting until the close of life before we die to sin. We have only to thoroughly let go of all selfish schemes and projects whatever, and give ourselves as absolutely up to the service of God, as much as we expect to when we come to die, and we enter at once into this infinitely desirable state of mind.

Once people have entered into this state of mind, new trials may call for fresh baptisms of the Holy Spirit. While we are in this world of temptation, we are never beyond the reach of sin and never out of danger. If selfishness could be called into exercise in holy Adam, how much more so in those who have lived so long under the dominion of selfishness? If a man has been intemperate or licentious, although these appetites and propensities may be subdued; still, it behooves him to keep out of temptation's way. Renewed temptations call for fresh and more powerful baptisms of the Holy Spirit. Be not satisfied then with one anointing of the Holy Spirit. Look day by day for deeper draughts of the water of life.

If we allow any form of sin to live, it will have dominion. We must wholly exterminate every form of sin or it will be our ruler. The principle of total abstinence in regard to sin is wholly indispensable to the reign of spiritual life.

Let us then, beloved, not rest satisfied until we are conscious that we are dead and buried by spiritual baptism into Christ's death; until we are planted in the likeness of His death and so crucified with Him that the body of death is fully destroyed.***

---

*James Brainerd Taylor (1801-1829), though only 28 years old when he died, he left an autobiography of more than 400 pages: *Memoirs of James Brainerd Taylor*, New York: American Tract Society, 1833.

**Edward Payson (1783-1827) an American clergyman, whose memoirs and sermons were quite popular in Finney's day, and remain so in our own time: *Payson's Complete Works*, Boston: Hyde, Lord, and Duren, 1846.

*** Charles G. Finney, "The Oberlin Evangelist," as "Death to Sin," July 15, 1840, as "The Nature of Death" in *Principles of Liberty*, 47–53. For Review: Answer the Study Questions on page 179, Cowles page 201.

9

Romans 6:7

The Psalms on Righteousness

Judgment will again be founded on righteousness, and all the upright in heart will follow it. —Psalm 94:15

They will sing before the LORD, for he comes, he comes to judge the earth. He will judge the world in righteousness and the peoples in his truth. —Psalm 96:13

Clouds and thick darkness surround him; righteousness and justice are the foundation of his throne. —Psalm 97:2

The LORD has made his salvation known and revealed his righteousness to the nations. —Psalm 98:2

He will judge the world in righteousness and the peoples with equity. —Psalm 98:9

The LORD works righteousness and justice for all the oppressed. —Psalm 103:6

But from everlasting to everlasting the LORD's love is with those who fear him, and his righteousness with their children's children—with those who keep his covenant and remember to obey his precepts. —Psalm 103:17-18

Glorious and majestic are his deeds, and his righteousness endures forever. —Psalm 111:3

Open for me the gates of righteousness; I will enter and give thanks to the LORD. —Psalm 118:19 (More on page 130)

10

Death to Sin through Christ
1853

Likewise reckon ye also yourselves to be dead indeed unto sin, but alive unto God through Jesus Christ our Lord.—Romans 6:11—KJV

In the same way, count yourselves dead to sin but alive to God in Christ Jesus.—Romans 6:11—NIV

The connection of other verses to this passage will help us understand its meaning. Near the close of Romans, chapter 5, Paul wrote, "The law entered that the offence might abound; but where sin abounded, grace did much more abound, that as sin hath reigned unto death, even so might grace reign through righteousness, unto eternal life, by Jesus Christ our Lord" (Romans 5:20, 21—KJV). He wrote of sin as a reigning principle or monarch, and of grace also as reigning. In chapter 6, he proceeded, "What shall we say then? Shall we continue in sin that grace may abound?" (Romans 6:1—KJV). Then, "Likewise reckon ye also yourselves to be dead indeed unto sin, but alive

125

unto God through Jesus Christ our Lord" (Romans 6:11—KJV). Now, observe that in Romans 6:6, Paul spoke of the old man, the old sinner, as being crucified with Christ: "Knowing this, that our old man is crucified with him, that the body of sin might be destroyed, that henceforth we should not serve sin?" Paul taught that the moral power of the cross so destroys the power of sin that the person who was once a sinner shall no longer serve sin. When he spoke of our being planted or buried with Christ, we must of course understand Paul as employing figures of speech to teach the great truth that the gospel redeems the soul from sin. As Christ died for our sin, so by a general analogy we die to sin; while on the other hand as He rose to a new and infinitely glorious life, so the convert rises to a new and blessed life of purity and holiness.

Returning particularly to our text, the language used in our translation would seem to denote that our death to sin is precisely analogous to Christ's death for sin; but this is not the case. We are dead to sin in the sense that it is no longer to be our Master, implying that it has been in power over us. However, sin never was in power over Jesus Christ—never was His master. Christ died to abolish its power over us—not to abolish any power of sin over himself, for it had none. The analogy between Christ's death in relation to sin and our dying to sin goes to this extent and no further: He died for the sake of making an atonement for sin and of creating a moral power that should be effective to kill the love of sin in all hearts. The Christian dies unto sin in the sense of being divorced from all sympathy with sin and of being emancipated from its control.

I shall discuss what it means to be dead unto sin. What it means to be alive unto God. What it means to reckon ourselves to be dead unto sin, but alive unto God through Jesus Christ our Lord. What the exhortation of our text implies.

What it means to be "dead to sin."

Being dead to sin must obviously be the opposite of being dead in sin. The latter must undeniably be a state of entire sinfulness—a state in which the soul is dead to all good through the power of sin over it. But right over against this, to be dead to sin must be to be indifferent to its attractions—beyond the reach of its influence—as fully removed from its influences as the dead are from the objects of sense in this world. As one who is dead in the natural sense has nothing more to do with earthly things, so one who is dead to sin has nothing to do any more with sin's attractions or with sinning itself.

What it means to be "alive to God."

To be alive unto God means to be full of life for Him—to be altogether active and on the alert to do His will—to make our whole lives a perpetual offering to Him, constantly delivering up ourselves to Him and His service that we may glorify His name and serve His interests.

What it means to reckon ourselves "dead to sin" and "alive to God."

To "reckon" sometimes means "account." Abraham's faith was reckoned or accounted unto him for righteousness. In this passage, "reckon" must mean to account, believe, or esteem yourself dead indeed unto sin. You account this to be the case. Regard this as truly your relation to sin: you are entirely dead to sin. Sin shall have no more dominion over you. A careful examination of the passages where this original word is used will show that this is its usual and natural sense. This gives the true idea of gospel faith, embracing personally the salvation which is by faith in Jesus Christ.

By reckoning yourself alive indeed unto God through Jesus Christ means that you expect to be saved by Jesus Christ and you calculate on this salvation as your own. You esteem yourself as wholly dead to sin and as consequently brought into life and peace in Christ Jesus.

The exhortation of our text implies that there is an adequate provision for this expectation, and for realizing these blessings in fact. If there were no ground for realizing this, the injunction would be most absurd. A precept requiring us to account ourselves dead indeed unto sin and alive unto God would be untenable if there were no probability of the thing—if no provision were made for our coming into such relations to sin on the one hand and to God through Christ on the other. If we could

10

Romans 6:11

127

not reasonably expect these blessings, there could be no rational ground for the expectation. If it were not reasonable to expect it, then to enjoin us to expect it would be palpably unreasonable. Who does not see that the very injunction implies that there is a foundation laid and adequate provision made for the state required?

Complying with this injunction implies believing such a thing to be possible. We must believe it possible that through Christ we may live in the required manner, that we may avoid sin—desist from sinning—give it up and abandon it altogether, and put it forever away. There can be no intelligent compliance with this precept unless this belief underlies its practicability. The mind must regard the state required as a practicable one—not merely as true in theory—not merely as good philosophy—but as actually made practicable by adequate grace, adapted to the laws of mind and to the actual moral condition of lost human beings.

We must cease from all expectation of attaining this state by ourselves, by our own independent, unaided efforts. We cannot begin to receive this by grace until we renounce all expectation of attaining this state by natural works. It is only when empty of self that we begin to be filled of Christ.

We must have a present willingness to be saved from sin. We must actually renounce all sin as such; that is, renounce sin because it is sin and for what it is. The mind must take this position: "I can have nothing more to do with sinning, for God hates sin and I am to live henceforth and forever to please and glorify Him. My soul is committed with its strength of purpose to this pleasing of God and doing His will."

We must entirely commit our whole case to Jesus Christ, not only for present but also for all future salvation from sin. This step must always be essential and vital—the cardinal act in this great work of salvation from sin.

We must foreclose the mind against temptation in such a sense that the mind truly expects to live a life purely devoted to God. This is the same sort of foreclosing of the mind as takes place under a faithful marriage contract. The Bible everywhere keeps this figure prominent. Christians are represented as the bride of Christ. They stand in a relation to Him, which is closely analogous to that of a bride to her husband. Hence, when they commit their whole hearts to Him, reposing their affections in Him and trusting Him for all good, their hearts are strongly foreclosed against temptation. We see the principle here involved illustrated in the merely human relationship. When parties are solemnly betrothed in mutual honest fidelity, there is no longer any thought of letting the eye rove or the heart go abroad for a fresh object of interest and love. The heart is fixed, willingly and by plighted faith fixed, and this fact shuts out the power of temptation almost entirely. It renders it comparatively an easy matter to keep the heart safely above the influence of temptation to apostasy. Before the sacred vows are taken, individuals may be excused for looking round and making any observations or enquiries, but never after the solemn vow is made. After the parties have become one by vow of marriage, never to be broken, there is to be no more question as to a better choice, no further thought about changing the relation or withdrawing the heart's affections. No wavering is admissible now; the pledge is made for everlasting faithfulness, settled once and forever! This is God's own illustration, and surely none need be more apt or more forcible. It shows how the Christian should look upon sin and upon all temptation to sin. He must say, "Away from my heart forever! I am married to Jesus Christ; how then can I look after other lovers? My mind is forever settled. It rests in the deep repose of one whose affections are plighted and fixed, to rove no more! Sin? I can think of yielding to its seductions no longer. I cannot entertain the question for a moment. I can have nothing to do with sinning. My mind is settled—the question forever foreclosed, and I can no more admit the temptation to small sins than to great sins—no more consent to give my heart to worldly idols than to commit murder! I did not enter upon the Christian faith as upon an experiment, to see how I might like it—no more than a wife or husband will take on themselves the marriage vow as an experiment. No. My whole soul has committed itself to Jesus Christ with as much expectation of being faithful forever as the most faithful husband and wife have of fulfilling their vows in all fidelity until death shall part them." Christians in this state of mind no more expect to commit small sins than great sins. Hating all sin for its own sake and for its hatefulness to Christ, any sin however small is to them as murder. Hence, if the heart is ever afterwards seduced and overcome by

10

Romans 6:11

temptation, it is altogether contrary to their expectation and purpose. It was not embraced in their plan by any means, but was distinctly excluded. It was not deliberately indulged aforetime, but broke on them unexpectedly through the vantage ground of old habits or associations.

The state of mind in question implies that the Christian knows where his great strength lies. He knows it does not lie in works of fasting, giving alms, making prayers, doing public duties or private duties—nothing of this sort—not even in resolutions or any self-originated efforts, but only in Christ received by faith. He no more expects spiritual life of himself apart from Christ than a man in his senses would expect to fly by swinging his arms in the air. Deep in his soul he knows that his whole strength lies in Christ alone.

When people are so enlightened as truly to apprehend this subject, then to expect less than this from Jesus Christ as the result of committing the whole soul to Him for full salvation is virtually to reject Him as a revealed Savior. It does not honor Him for what He is. It does not honor the revelations He has made of himself in His word by accepting Him as presented there. Consider the first element of this salvation. It is not being saved from hell, but being saved from sin. In every sense, salvation from punishment is quite a secondary thing. Salvation from punishment is only a result of being saved from sin, and not the prime element in gospel salvation. Why was the infant Messiah to be called Jesus? Because He should save His people from their sins. Does the Bible anywhere teach any other or different view from this?

REMARKS

This text alone, "Reckon yourselves to be dead indeed unto sin, but alive unto God through Jesus Christ" most entirely justifies the expectation of living without sin through all-abounding grace. If there were no other passage bearing on this point, this alone is adequate, and for a Christian to offer this only as a reason for such a hope in Him is to offer as good a reason as need be given. Many other verses also fully justify this expectation.

To teach that such an expectation is a dangerous error is to teach un-

belief. What if the Apostle Paul had added to this injunction (which requires us to account ourselves dead indeed unto sin but alive unto God)
this singular averment: "Yet let me warn you, nobody can rationally hope
to be free from sin in this world. You must remember that to entertain
such an expectation as God enjoins in this language is a dangerous error."
What should we think of this, if it followed Romans 6:11, as a verse?

No one can deny that the passage treats of sanctification. The whole
question is shall Christians "continue in sin" after having been forgiven
and accepted in their Redeemer. Paul labors to show that they should
and may die to sin—even as Christ died for sin. Christians may also live
a new, a spiritual life (through faith in His grace), even as Christ lives a
higher and more glorious life.

Let me refer here to some other verses in the Bible. "Be not unequally
yoked with unbelievers—what agreement hath the temple of God with
idols? For ye are the temple of the living God. Wherefore come out from
among them and be ye separate, saith the Lord, and touch not the un-
clean thing, and I will receive you, and will be a Father unto you and ye
shall be my sons and daughters, saith the Lord Almighty" (2 Corinthians
6:14-18—KJV). And, "Having therefore these promises, dearly beloved,
let us cleanse ourselves from all filthiness of the flesh and of the spirit, per-
fecting holiness in the fear of God" (2 Corinthians 7:1—KJV). These are
very remarkable verses. Note how precept and promise are intermingled,
and how, finally, upon the basis of a most glorious promise is founded
the precept enjoining us to perfect holiness. What should we think of
the Apostle Paul (and of the Divine Spirit who spoke through Paul), if he
had immediately added to these verses, "Take care lest any of you should
be led by these remarks to indulge the very dangerous and erroneous expectation that you can 'perfect holiness,' or 'cleanse yourselves from any
sin, either of flesh or spirit, in this world.'" Would not this have been
trifling with the intelligence and Christian sensibility of every reader of
his words through all time? Should we not account such an addition as
substantially blasphemous?

The Bible never gainsays its own teachings. However, I ask, "What if
it did?" What if the Bible had solemnly asserted, "No mere human being
either of himself or by any grace received in this life has ever kept or shall

10

Romans 6:11

ever keep the commandments of God wholly, but daily breaks them in thought, word, and deed?" To teach that such an expectation is dangerous is a great deal worse than no teaching at all. It would be better to leave people to their own unaided reading of God's word. Dangerous?! What does this mean? What! Dangerous to expect victory over any sin? If so, what is the gospel worth? What gospel have we that can be deemed good news at all?

Many indulge the very opposite expectation. Far from expecting any such thing as the apostle authorizes them to expect, they know they have no such expectation. Still more than this is true of some people. They expect to count themselves always in sin. They depend on reckoning themselves not dead indeed unto sin but somewhat alive to it through all their mortal life, and in part alive to God through Jesus Christ. It follows as quite a thing of course that expecting no such thing as complete victory over sin, they will use no appropriate means, since faith stands foremost among those means, and faith must include at least a confidence that the thing sought is possible to be attained.

In this, we have the essence of the good news of the gospel. Any one who has been wounded and made sore by sin—its bitter shafts sinking deep into his moral being—one who has known its bitterness and felt the poison thereof drink up his spirit—such a one will see that there is glory in the idea of being delivered from sin. He will surely see that this deliverance is by far the greatest need of his soul, and that nothing can be compared with escaping from this body of sin and death. Look at the seventh chapter of Romans. There you will have the state of a man who is more than convinced, who is really convicted, of sin. It is one thing to be *convinced* of sin, and a yet further stage of progress in the right direction to be *convicted* of sin. This term implies the agency of another party. The criminal at the bar may be quite convinced of his guilt by the view he was compelled to take of his own case; but his being convicted is a still further step; the testimony and the jury convict him.

Some of you know what it is to see yourself a sinner, and yet the sight of the fact brings with it no smart—no sting. It does not cut deep into your very soul. On the other hand, some of you may know what it is to see your sins all armed like an armed man to pierce you through and through with

132

daggers. Then you cry out, "O wretched man that I am! Who shall deliver me from the body of this death?" (Romans 7:24—KJV). You feel a piercing sting as if your soul were filled with poison—with dark rankling venom diffusing through the depths of your soul the very agonies of hell! This is what I mean by being convicted, as a state of mind beyond being merely convinced. The shafts and the smiting of sin seem really like the piercing of an arrow, as if arrows from the Almighty did really drink up your spirit. When you experience this, then you can understand what the good news of the gospel is. A remedy for such pangs must be good news beyond all contradiction. Then to know that the blood of Christ can save is indeed a cordial of life to the fainting soul.

Place a person in this state of cutting, piercing conviction, and then let him feel that there is actually no remedy, and he sinks under the iron shafts of despair. See his agony! Tell him there can never be any remedy for his guilty soul! You must lie there in your wailing and despair forever! Can any state of mind be more awful?

I remember a case that occurred in Reading, Pennsylvania many years ago. There was a man of hard heart and iron frame, a strong burly man, who had stood up against the revival as if he could shake off all the arrows of the Almighty, even as the Mastodon of which the tradition of the red man says, he shook off all the arrows of the warriors from his brow and felt no harm. So he stood. But he had a praying wife and a praying sister, and they gathered their souls in the might of prayer close about him as a party of men would hem in a wild bull in a net. Soon it was apparent that an arrow from the quiver of the Almighty had pierced between the joints of his harness and had taken hold of his innermost heart. O, was not he in agony then! It was night, dark, and intensely cold. It seemed that absolutely he could not live. They sent for me to come and see him. I went. While yet sixty rods from his house I heard his screams and wailings of woe. It made me feel very solemn, so like the echoes of the pit of hell! I reached the house: there he lay on the floor rolling in his agony and wailing, as is rarely heard this side the pit of despair. Cold as the weather was, he sweat like rain, every part of his frame being in a most intense perspiration. O, his groans! And to see him gnaw his very tongue for pain—this could not but give one some idea of the doom of the damned. "O," said I,

10

Romans 6:11

133

"If this be only conviction, what is hell?!" But he could not bear to hear anything about sin. His conscience was already full of it, and had brought out the awful things of God's law so as to leave nothing more to be done in that direction. I could only put Christ before him, and just hold his mind to the view of Christ alone. This soon brought relief. However, suppose I had nothing else to say but this, "Mr. B., there is no help possible for your case! You can wail on and wail on: no being in the universe can help you?" Need you say to him hell has no fire? O, he has fire enough in his burning soul already. It seems to him that no hell of fire can possibly be worse than this.

How perfectly chilling and horrible for people to oppose the idea of expecting deliverance from sin and yet talk calmly of going on in sin all the rest of their earthly days! An elder whom I knew rose in a meeting and told the Lord that he had been living in sin thus far and expected to go on in sin as long as he lived. He said he had sinned today and should doubtless sin tomorrow and so on. Yet, he talked as calmly about it all as if it were foolish to make any ado, as well as impossible to attempt any change for the better. Talk of all this calmly! Think of that! Quite calmly of living along in sin all the rest of his days! How horrible! Suppose a wife should say to her husband, "I love you some, but you know I love many other men too, and I find it pleasant to indulge myself with them. You certainly must be aware that all women are frail creatures and liable to fall continually, and indeed you know that I expect to fall more or less as it may happen every day I live, so that you certainly will not expect from me anything so impracticable and fanatical as unblemished virtue! You know we have none of us any idea of being perfect in the present life. We don't believe in any such thing!" Now let me ask you to look at this woman and hear what she has to say. Can you hear her talk so without having your soul filled with horror? What! Is this woman a wife, and does she think and talk in this way about conjugal fidelity?

And yet, this is not to be compared in shocking guilt and treason with the case of the Christian who says, "I expect to sin every day I live," and who says this with unmoved carelessness? You expect to be a traitor to Jesus each day of your life—to crucify Him afresh every day. You expect to put Him each day to an open shame; each day to dishonor His name, and grieve His heart, and to bring sorrow and shame upon all who love Christ's cause; and yet you talk about having a good hope through grace! But tell me, does not every true Christian say, "Do not let me live at all if I cannot live without sin; for how can I bear to go on day by day sinning against Him whom I love so much!"

Those who are opposed to this idea are either very ignorant of what the gospel is, or they are impenitent and of course do not care to be delivered from their sins; or at best they are guilty of great unbelief. Into which of these classes the opposers of the doctrine may fall is a question for themselves to settle, as between their own consciences and their God.

There are two distinct views of salvation entertained among professed Christians, and correspondingly two distinct classes of professing Christians often embraced within the same church. The one class regards the gospel as a salvation from sin. They think more of this and value it more than the hope of heaven, or of earth either. The great thing with them is to realize the idea of deliverance from sin. This constitutes the charm and glory of the gospel. They seek this more than to be saved from hell. They care more by far to be saved from sin itself than from its penal consequences. Of the latter they think and pray but little. It is their glory and their joy that Christ is sent to deliver them from their bondage in iniquity, to lift them up from their wretched state and give them the liberty of love. This they labor to realize; this is to them the good news of gospel salvation.

The other class of professing Christians is mostly anxious to be saved from hell. The punishment due for sin is the thing they chiefly fear. In fact, fear has been mainly the spring of their religious efforts. The gospel is not thought of as a means of deliverance from sin, but as a great system of indulgences—a vast accommodation to take off the fear and danger of damnation, while yet it leaves them in their sin. Now, here I do not by any means imply that they will call their system of gospel faith a scheme of indulgences: the name doubtless will be an offence to them. They may not have distinctly considered this point, and may have failed to notice that in fact it is such and nothing better. They seem not to notice that a scheme of salvation that removes the fear of damnation for sin, and which leaves them in their sins to live for themselves to please themselves,

10

Romans 6:11

and which holds that Christ will at last bring them to heaven notwithstanding their having lived in sin all their days, must be a vast scheme of indulgences. Indeed, it is a compromise on a most magnificent scale. By virtue of it, the whole church is expected to wallow on in sin through life, and be none the less sure of heaven at last.

These opposite views are so prevalent and so palpable you will see them everywhere as you go around among the churches. You will find many in the church who are altogether worldly and selfish; who live conformed to the world in various neglects of duty, and who expect to indulge themselves in sin more or less all the way through life. You may ask them, "Do you think that is right?" They will answer, "No." "Why then do you do it?" "O, we are all imperfect, and we can't expect to be any better than imperfect while here in the flesh." Yet they expect to be saved at last from hell and to have all their sins forgiven; but how? Not on condition of sincerely turning away from all their sins, but on the assumption that the gospel is a vast system of indulgences—more vast by far than Pope Leo X ever wielded and worked to comfort sinning professing Christians in his day. For here, not merely those who sin occasionally as there, but those who live in sin and know they do, and expect they shall as long as they live, yet expect to be saved without fail at last.

The other class of professing Christians has no expectation of being saved unless as they have a pure heart and live above the world. Talk to them about living in sin; they hate and dread the very thought. To them the poison of asps is in it. Sin is bitter to their souls. They dread it as they dread death itself.

No one can go around within this church or any other without finding these two classes as distinct in their apprehension of the gospel as I have described them to be. The one class are in agony if they find themselves even slipping, and they are specially cautious against exposing themselves to temptation.

Not so with the other class. Two ministers of the gospel being together, one urged the other strongly to engage in a certain service. The other declined. "Why not go?" said the first. He replied, "Because I do not think myself justified in exposing myself to such and so much temptation." "But why stop for that? We expect to sin more or less always; and all we have to do is to repent of it afterwards." Horror-smitten, the other could only say, "I hold to a different gospel from that altogether."

Suppose a wife should say to her husband, "I am determined I will go to the theater." "But, my dear," says he, "you know bad people congregate there, and you may be tempted." But she replies, "Never mind; if I sin, I will repent of it afterwards."

The real Christian may be known by this, that the very thought of being drawn into sin drives him to agony. He cannot bear the idea of living in sin, no, not for one moment.

Young people who are truly Christians are careful about their vacations. They will be on their guard, for they do not want to be trapped into sin. I do not mean that they need fear to go where God calls them, but it is a terrible thing to be ensnared into sin, and they cannot but feel it to be so. If you know what it is to be wounded by the arrows of sin in your soul, you will go abroad into apparent danger, walking softly and with caution, and much prayer. You will surely be much on your guard. But if you say, "O, if I sin I will repent," what shall I say of you? You will repent, will you? And this will make it all right again so easily? Suppose you foresaw that in going abroad for vacation, you would get drunk a few times, and would commit one or two murders, would you say, "O, I may be a good Christian notwithstanding. I will be careful to repent of it after it is all over." Horrible! And yet you can think yourself a good Christian! Let me tell you, a Christian who repents of sin, repents of it as sin. He makes no such discriminations as between a little secret sin and a great sin, for example, a murder. He knows no such distinction between sins as will leave him to commit the one class without scruple and to shrink from the other. With him, anything that grieves God is a horrible thing. Anything that displeases God is a sin. "Ah," he cries out, "God will see it! It will grieve His heart!" How it will affect God—this is overall with him. One who knows what it is to appear guilty of sin before God, and then who knows also what it is to be delivered from this condition, will understand how the Christian ought to feel in circumstances of temptation, where he feels himself in danger of sinning. His hair all stands on end! How awful to sin against God! Hence, anything that seems likely to bring him into danger will rouse up all his soul within him and put him on his guard.

10

Romans 6:11

The unbelief of the church as to what they may receive from Christ is the great stumbling block, hindering themselves and others from experiencing deliverance. Not only is this a great curse to professing Christians, but it is also a great grief to Jesus Christ and a sore trial.

Many seem to have hardened their hearts against all expectation of this deliverance from sin. They have heard the doctrine preached. They have seen some profess to be in this state of salvation from sin, but they have also seen some of this class fall again, and now they deliberately reject the whole doctrine. But is this consistent with really embracing the gospel? What is Christ to the believer? What was His errand into the world? What is He doing and what is He trying to do? He has come to break the power of sin in the heart, and to be the life of the believer, working in him a perpetual salvation from sin, aiming to bring him thus, and only thus, to heaven at last.

What is faith? Faith is actually giving yourself to Christ that He may do this work for you and in you! What are you to believe of Christ if not this, that He is to save His people from their sins? Can you tell of anything else? Does the Bible tell you to expect something different and less than this? The fact is, it has been the great stumbling block to the church that this thing has not been well understood. The common experience of nominal Christians has misrepresented and belied the truth. The masses forming their views much more from this experience than from the Bible, or at best applying this experience to interpret the Bible, have adopted exceedingly defective, not to say false, opinions as to the nature and design of the gospel. They seem to forget altogether that Paul writing to Christians at Rome assures them that if they are under grace, sin shall not have dominion over them.

When Christians do not expect this blessing from Christ, they will not get it. While they expect so little as they usually do, no wonder they get so little. According to their faith, and not ever very much beyond it, need they expect to receive.

It is often the case that sanctification is held as a theory, while the mind does not yet by any means embrace the truth in love. The case is analogous to that of impenitent sinners who hold in theory that they must have a new heart. They profess to believe this. But do they really understand it? No. Suppose it were revealed to their minds so that they should really see it as it is, would they not see a new thing? Would they not be startled to see how utterly far they are, while impenitent, from being acceptable to God, and how great the change they must experience before they can enter the kingdom? So of sanctification. Although this class of persons profess to hold it in theory, yet the passages of Scripture which describe it do not enter into their experience. They do not see the whole truth. If they were to see the whole truth, and should then reject it, I believe it would be in them the unpardonable sin. When the Spirit of God discloses to them the real meaning of the gospel, then if they deliberately reject it, how can the sin be less than what the Scriptures represent as the unpardonable sin? Having once been enlightened and having received the knowledge of the truth that they might be saved, then turning back, is it not thenceforth impossible that they should be renewed again to repentance? One thing, at least, must be said, there is a peril which many of those professing to be Christians seem not to realize in having so much light before the mind as they actually have in regard to the provisions made in the gospel for present sanctification, and then in rejecting this light practically and living still in sin as if the gospel made no provision to save the Christian from his sins. Into this awful peril how many rush blindly and to their own destruction!*

---

* Charles G. Finney, "The Oberlin Evangelist," September 14, 1853, *Sermons on Gospel Themes*, 380–397, *Principles of Victory*, 63–73. For Review: Answer the Study Questions on page 180, Cowles page 202.

10

Romans 6:11

The Psalms on Righteousness

How I long for your precepts! Preserve my life in your righteousness.—Psalm 119:40

Your righteousness is everlasting and your law is true.—Psalm 119:142

May your priests be clothed with righteousness; may your saints sing for joy.—Psalm 132:9

O LORD, hear my prayer, listen to my cry for mercy; in your faithfulness and righteousness come to my relief.—Psalm 143:1

For your name's sake, O LORD, preserve my life; in your righteousness, bring me out of trouble.—Psalm 143:11

They will celebrate your abundant goodness and joyfully sing of your righteousness.—Psalm 145:7

The Proverbs on Righteousness

I walk in the way of righteousness, along the paths of justice.—Proverbs 8:20

Ill-gotten treasures are of no value, but righteousness delivers from death.—Proverbs 10:2

The righteousness of the blameless makes a straight way for them, but the wicked are brought down by their own wickedness. The righteousness of the upright delivers them, but the unfaithful are trapped by evil desires.—Proverbs 11:5-6 (More on page 142)

11

Sanctification Under Grace
1839

For sin shall not have dominion over you: for ye are not under the law, but under grace. —Romans 6:14—KJV

For sin shall not be your master, because you are not under law, but under grace. —Romans 6:14—NIV

Sin is a state of mind which is the opposite of the law of God. As I have shown, in a former lecture, the whole of true Christianity consists in obedience to the law of God, *which requires supreme disinterested love to God and disinterested and equal love to our neighbor.* This is the opposite of selfishness or a supreme regard to our own interest. Selfishness therefore, under all its forms, is sin. All sin is some modification of selfishness. Sin is not any part of our physical or mental constitution. Sin is no part or principle of human nature itself, but a voluntary state of mind. Sin is an action or choice of the mind, a preferring our own interest because it is our own to other and higher interests. It does not consist in any defect of our human nature. Sin is a perversion or prohibited use of our human nature.

Sin does not have dominion of your life, just because you have fallen under the power of an occasional temptation. Some suppose this passage to teach that a person under grace could not sin under any circumstances. They maintain that to sin once is to come under the dominion of sin. Although I am for making God's promises mean all they say, I do not believe they mean all that some interpret them to mean. For example, if a person became intoxicated once, under circumstances of peculiar temptation, it would be neither fair, nor true, in speaking of his general character, to say that he was under the dominion of ardent spirits and a slave to his appetite.

To illustrate my meaning, consider the parallel promise in John 4:14. Christ says, "But whosoever drinketh the water, that I shall give him, shall never thirst; but the water, that I shall give him, shall be in him a well of water springing up into everlasting life." Some have understood this promise to mean that if a person became a partaker of the Holy Spirit, he could never again know what it was to thirst for the divine influence in any sense. They argue that the person would have such a fullness of the Spirit of God that they would never have any thirsting for more. This is certainly a forced construction of this passage. It is not in accordance with what we would mean in the use of similar language. If you told your neighbor that if he boarded with you, he would never hunger or thirst, would he understand you to mean that he would never have a good appetite. Or, would he merely understand that he would not be hungry or thirsty without being supplied with food and drink? He would doubtless understand you, and you would expect him to understand you, to promise that he would always have enough to eat and drink, that he should not suffer the pain of hunger or thirst without the supply that nature demands. In this way, I understand this promise of Christ. If anyone partakes of the waters of life that Christ offers, Christ has pledged that he shall have as great a measure of His Spirit as he needs or his necessities demand. Whenever his soul thirsts for more of the waters of life, he has a right to plead this promise in prayer with an assurance that Christ will satisfy his thirsty soul with living waters.

I suppose Paul's words in our text have a similar meaning. He does not mean that a believer under temptation cannot fall under the power of an occasional sin. He means that *no form of sin shall be habitual.* No form of selfishness or lust shall be habitual in the person who is under grace. No appetite, or passion, or temptation of any kind will be able to bring the person under grace into bondage to sin.

What it means to be under the law.

To be under the law is to be subject to the law as a covenant of works. In other words, to be under the law is to be under the necessity of perfectly fulfilling the law in order to obtain salvation. To be under the law is to be influenced by legal motives or considerations, to be constrained by the fear of punishment or influenced by the hope of reward. To be under the law is to be constrained by conscience and a sense of duty, instead of by love. Individuals seem to go painfully about their duty under the biddings of conscience, and submit with about as much pain and reluctance as a slave to his master.

To be under the law is to be under the condemning sentence of the law, like a state criminal, and of course shut out from communion with God. A state criminal, under sentence, is legally shut out from all friendly intercourse with the government and is considered and treated as an outlaw. Just so with a sinner, under the sentence of God's law. While the sinner remains in a state of spiritual death and alienation from God, the sentence of eternal death is out against him. He is shut out from communion with God; consequently, sin will have dominion over him.

What it means to be under grace.

We need to distinguish being under a covenant of grace from being under a covenant of law. By a covenant of grace, I mean the covenant that confers all the blessings of salvation as a mere gratuity. Even more than a gratuity, the blessings we receive are the direct opposite of our deserts.

Under the covenant of grace, love influences the believer and he is excited and moved by grace and not by legal motives. Living under the

11

Romans 6:14

143

covenant of grace is to be put in possession of the blessings of the new, gracious covenant as God spoke through Jeremiah, "Behold, the days come, saith the LORD, that I will make a new covenant with the house of Israel, and with the house of Judah: Not according to the covenant that I made with their fathers in the day that I took them by the hand to bring them out of the land of Egypt; which my covenant they brake, although I was an husband unto them, saith the LORD: But this shall be the covenant that I will make with the house of Israel; After those days, saith the LORD, I will put my law in their inward parts, and write it in their hearts; and will be their God, and they shall be my people. And they shall teach no more every man his neighbor, and every man his brother, saying, Know the LORD: for they shall all know me, from the least of them unto the greatest of them, saith the LORD; for I will forgive their iniquity, and I will remember their sin no more" (Jeremiah 31:31-34).

In addition, in the Letter to the Hebrews, we read, "For finding fault with them, he saith, Behold, the days come, saith the Lord, when I will make a new covenant with the house of Israel and with the house of Judah: Not according to the covenant that I made with their fathers in the day when I took them by the hand to lead them out of the land of Egypt; because they continued not in my covenant, and I regarded them not, saith the Lord. For this is the covenant that I will make with the house of Israel after those days, saith the Lord; I will put my laws into their mind, and write them in their hearts: and I will be to them a God, and they shall be to me a people: And they shall not teach every man his neighbor, and every man his brother, saying, Know the Lord: for all shall know me, from the least to the greatest. For I will be merciful to their unrighteousness, and their sins and their iniquities will I remember no more. In that he saith, A new covenant, he hath made the first old. Now that which decayeth and waxeth old is ready to vanish away" (Hebrews 8:8-13—KJV).

To be under grace is to be united to Christ by faith and to receive a continual life and influence from Him. He compares himself to a vine and His children as the branches. To be under grace is to be united to Him as a branch is united to the vine, so as to receive our continual support, strength, nourishment and life from Him.

To be under grace is to pass from death unto life, to be translated from the kingdom of darkness into the kingdom of God's dear Son; to pass from the state of a condemned criminal into a state of redemption, justification, and adoption.

The dominion of sin and the deliverance from sin.

Under the law, sin will have dominion over an unsanctified mind, because this is the certain effect of the law upon a selfish mind. A selfish mind is naturally seeking its own interests. If it attempts to obey the law, it will be through selfish considerations, through hope or fear. In every such attempt, the mind must naturally fail; for the law prohibits selfishness. Every attempt to obey the law from selfish motives is only a grievous breach of the law. If God canceled all former sins, and if salvation depended upon future obedience to the law, salvation would be forever impossible. If the mind attempted to obey for the sake of obtaining salvation, this would be selfishness and disobedience. In every such attempt, the mind must naturally fail.

Sin must have dominion over a selfish mind that is under law, or it would amount to this absurdity, that the disinterested love demanded by the law would flow from selfish motives—a thing naturally impossible.

To produce disinterested love, salvation must be gratuitous. The soul must understand that legal obedience to the law is not the condition to salvation, for if it understood legal obedience to be the condition of salvation, it is impossible that this consideration should not influence a selfish mind in its efforts to obey. This consideration would render all attempts at obedience ineffectual and sin would continue to have dominion.

Selfishness will of course seek present and selfish gratification until compelled by deep conviction to desist. In which case, the will certainly takes refuge in a self-righteous attempt to obey the law, unless it understands that salvation is gratuitous or a matter of grace. There seems to be, as a matter of fact, no other way in which the power of selfishness can be broken except to annihilate the reasons for selfish efforts by bringing home to the soul the truth that salvation is by grace through faith.

The Apostle Paul in the Seventh Chapter of Romans beautifully illustrates the effect of law upon a selfish mind. The case there supposed is what the Apostle, as is common with him, represents as if it were his own experience. It appears, from its connection, to illustrate the influence of God's law over an unsanctified mind. *It is plainly a case where sin was habitual, where sin had dominion*, where the law of sin and death in the members so warred against the law of the mind as to bring the soul into captivity. Now some have contended, and continue to contend, that the Apostle, in this chapter, describes the experience of a saint under grace. However, this cannot be because, in this case, it would flatly contradict the text upon which I am preaching. As I have said, the case described in the Seventh Chapter of Romans is a case in which sin undeniably has dominion, the very thing of which the Apostle complains. However, the text affirms that sin shall not have dominion over the soul that is under grace. Besides, it is very plain, that in the Seventh Chapter of Romans it was the influence of the law, and not of grace, which the Apostle was discussing.

Another reason why sin will have dominion under the law is that under the law people are left to the unaided exercise of their own powers of moral agency. They do not have those gracious helps which alone can induce true holiness. The law throws out its claims upon them and requires the perfect use and entire consecration of all their powers to the service of God. Then the law leaves them to obey or disobey at their peril. The law neither secures nor promises to them any aid. The law requires them to go forth to the service of God, to love God with all their heart and their neighbor as themselves on pain of death. Now in such circumstances it is very plain that a mind already selfish will only be confirmed in selfishness under such a dispensation.

Sin cannot have dominion over those who are under grace, because the law is written in their hearts—the spirit of the law has taken possession of their souls and made believers forever "free from the law of sin and death," which was in our members.

Sin cannot have dominion over those who are under grace, because the soul has become acquainted with God, and with Christ, and has fallen deeply in love with their character. The soul delights in God and exercises the very temper required by the law, uninfluenced by the hope of its rewards or by the fear of its penalty. The believer is overcome and swallowed up with the love that naturally results from a right acquaintance with God. Now in this state of mind, sin can no longer have dominion over the soul—no form of selfishness can be habitual any more than a wife, who loves her husband supremely, can become a habitual adulterer. A woman who loves her husband, might, by force of circumstances, and by some unexpected and powerful temptation, be led to sin against her husband; but for this to become habitual, while the supreme love of her husband continues, is a contradiction.

Sin cannot have dominion over the soul, because Christ has become its life. He is represented not only as the Life of the soul, but also as the Head of the Church, and Christians as members of His body, and flesh, and bones. Now as the vine supplies the branch, and as the head controls the members, so Christ has become the main-spring—the well spring of life in the soul; and sin cannot have dominion over such a soul, unless it can have dominion over Christ. Christ may find it necessary to permit the soul to fall into an occasional sin, to teach it by experience what perhaps it will not learn in any other way. However, it cannot be necessary that occasional sin should become habitual to give the soul a sense of its dependence; and Christ, by express promise, has secured the soul against it.

Sin cannot have dominion over the soul, because the soul so reposes in the blood of Christ for justification and salvation as to have no motive to selfish efforts, being released from the responsibility of working out a legal righteousness. It is constrained by such a sense of abundant and overflowing grace that it loves and serves God, having no reason to serve itself.

Sin cannot have dominion over the soul, because it is so constrained by a sense of the love of Christ as to be as unable to indulge in sin, and vastly more so, than the most dutiful and affectionate child is to indulge in habitual and willful disobedience to its parents.

It is impossible for sin to have dominion over a Christian, because it implies a contradiction. *To be a Christian is habitually to love, serve, and honor God.* Obedience is the rule, and sin is the exception. It is therefore impossible that sin should have dominion over a Christian, for this

11

Romans 6:14

would be the same as to say that a person might be a Christian while sin was his rule and obedience the exception; or, in other words, that sin is habitual, and obedience only occasional. If this is the definition of a Christian, then I know not what a Christian is.

Sin cannot have dominion, because the God of truth has pledged that sin shall not have dominion. Sin cannot have dominion, because the very terms of the covenant of grace show that to be under grace is to have the law written in the heart—to be made or rendered obedient to God by the residence of the Spirit of Christ within us.

Sin cannot have dominion, because every form of sin is hateful to the soul. Sin can have no influence except during a moment of strong temptation—when the involuntary powers, or emotions, are so strongly excited by temptation as to gain a momentary ascendancy over the will; while the deep preference of the mind, although for the time being comparatively inefficient, yet remains unchanged.

Sin cannot have dominion, because the soul under grace is led by the Holy Spirit to such an understanding and use of its powers as to make the soul a partaker of the Divine nature. John says, a person "born of God, doth not commit sin; for his seed remaineth in him" (1 John 3:9—KJV): the Spirit of Christ dwelling in him renders it unnatural for him to sin.

Sin cannot have dominion, because old things are passed away and all things are become new. The grand leading design of the mind has undergone a radical change. As the leading design of the mind must of course control the habitual conduct of the soul, and as deviations from its influence will only be occasional, and not habitual, so the soul under grace will not and cannot be under the dominion of sin.

REMARKS

There is no sound Christianity where there is not universal reformation. Constantly and strictly observe, in all cases of professed conversion, whether the reformation in habits and life is universal —whether it extends to selfishness, and sinful lusts, and habits of every kind, and under every form. If any lust is spared, if selfishness, under any form, is indulged, and habitual, if any sinful habit still remains unbroken and unsubdued, that is not a sound conversion. No form of sin will have dominion where conversion is real. Occasional sin may occur through the force of powerful temptation; but no form of sin will be indulged habitually.

Lack of attention to this truth has allowed a great many unconverted people to enter the church. In some respects, a reformation of life has been apparent, but without sufficient discrimination, the individual has indulged a hope of salvation and has been encouraged by members of the church. He has been admitted to the communion to the great disgrace of Christianity. It does not appear to me to have been sufficiently understood that grace not only ought, but actually does, in every case where piety is real, so overcome sin as to leave no form of it habitual. It has indeed been a common maxim that where sin is habitual, there is no real Christian faith. However, obviously, the church has not adopted this in practice; for great multitudes have been admitted to the church, and are still permitted to continue as members in good standing in Christian churches, who habitually indulge in many forms of sin. I think the gospel demands that no professed convert should be thus encouraged to hope, or allowed to become a member of the church, whose reformation of life and habits is not universal.

You see that all those people who have frequent convictions and conflicts with sin and yet are habitually overcome by sin are still under the law and not under grace. They are convicted, but not converted. The difficulty is their hearts are not changed so as to hate sin under every form. Temptation is too strong, therefore, for their conscience, and for all their resolutions. Their hearts pleading for indulgence will of course render them an easy prey to temptation. This seems to have been exactly the case described in the Seventh Chapter of Romans, to which I have referred. Where regeneration has taken place—and the heart, as well as the conscience has become opposed to sin—in every such case the power of temptation is, of course, so broken as that sin will at most be only occasional and never habitual. In all cases, therefore, where individuals find themselves to be, or are seen by others to be, under the dominion of sin or lust of any kind, they should know, or be told at once, that they have not been regenerated. They are under the law, and not under grace.

What can those people think of themselves, who know that they are

11

Romans 6:14

under the dominion of selfishness in some of its forms? Do they believe this text to be a direct and palpable falsehood? If not, how can they indulge the hope that they are Christians? This text asserts, as plainly as it can, that they are under the law, and not under grace.

You see the state of those who are encouraged by the Seventh Chapter of Romans, who suppose that to be a Christian's experience. If they have gone no further than that, they are still under the law. I have been amazed to see how pertinaciously those who profess to be Christians will cling to a legal experience, and justify themselves in it, by a reference to this Seventh Chapter of Romans. I am fully convinced that the modern construction of the chapter—from the 14th to the 25th verses—interpreting it as a Christian experience has done incalculable evil. It has led thousands of souls there to rest, and go no further, imagining that they are already as deeply versed in Christian experience as Paul was, when he wrote that epistle. There they have stayed, and hugged their delusion, till they have found themselves in the depths of hell.

There may be much legal reformation, without any true Christian faith. A legal reformation, however, may generally be distinguished, by some of the following marks: It may be only partial. It may extend to certain forms of sin, while others are indulged. It may and almost certainly will be temporary.

In a legal experience, it will also generally be obvious that some forms of sinful indulgence are practiced and defended as not being sin. Where there has not been a powerful conviction that has deterred the soul from indulgence, selfishness and lust are still tolerated.

A gospel or gracious experience will manifest itself in a universal hatred of sin and lust in every form. And, as I have said, sin will have no place, except in cases of such powerful temptation as to carry the will for the time, by the force of excited feelings; then, a reaction will immediately take place and the soul be prostate in the depths of repentance.

By reference to this text, and the principles here inculcated, not only may the genuineness of each pretended conversion be decided, but also the genuineness or spuriousness of religious excitements. That is not a revival of true religion, but falls entirely short of it, that does not produce universal reformation of habits in the subjects of it. There may be many revivals of the conviction of sin; convictions of sin that are often deep and very general in a community, where, for want of sufficient discriminating instruction, there are very few conversions.

You see the mistake of those sinners who fear to embrace Christianity, lest they should disgrace it by living in sin, as they see many professing Christians now doing.

Sinner, you need not stand back on this account. Only come out from under the law, and be truly converted. If you submit yourself to the power and influence of sovereign grace, no form of sin shall have dominion over you, as God is true.

This text is a great encouragement to real Christians. They often tremble when they have once fallen under the power of a temptation. They greatly fear that sin will gain an entire ascendancy over them.

Christian, lift up your head, and proclaim yourself free. The God of truth has declared that you are not and shall not be a slave to sin.

This is a proper promise, and an important one, for Christians to plead in prayer. It is like a sheet anchor in a storm. If temptations beat like a tempest upon the soul, let the Christian hold on to this promise with all his heart. Let him cry out, "O Lord, perform the good word of Thy grace unto Thy servant, wherein Thou hast caused me to hope that sin shall not have dominion over me, because I am not under law but under grace."

Let those who are under the law, over whom sin in any form has dominion, remember, that under the law there is no salvation. Whatever things the law says, it says to those who are under the law, and "cursed is every one that continueth not in all things written in the book of the law to do them" (Galatians 3:10—KJV).*

11

Romans 6:14

* Charles G. Finney, "The Oberlin Evangelist," April 24, 1839, untitled, but titled "Gospel Freedom" in the Index. "Sanctification Under Grace" is the title supplied by Timothy L. Smith, editor of *The Promise of the Spirit*, 117–124, which I also used as the title in *Principles of Liberty*, 55–63. For Review: Answer the Study Questions on page 181, Cowles page 202.

The Proverbs on Righteousness

The wicked man earns deceptive wages, but he who sows righteousness reaps a sure reward. —Proverbs 11:18

In the way of righteousness there is life; along that path is immortality. —Proverbs 12:28

Righteousness guards the man of integrity, but wickedness overthrows the sinner. —Proverbs 13:6

Righteousness exalts a nation, but sin is a disgrace to any people. — Proverbs 14:34

The LORD detests the way of the wicked but he loves those who pursue righteousness. —Proverbs 15:9

Better a little with righteousness than much gain with injustice. — Proverbs 16:8

Kings detest wrongdoing, for a throne is established through righteousness. —Proverbs 16:12

He who pursues righteousness and love finds life, prosperity and honor. —Proverbs 21:21

Remove the dross from the silver, and out comes material for the silversmith; remove the wicked from the king's presence, and his throne will be established through righteousness. —Proverbs 25:4-5 (More on page 160)

12

The Wages of Sin
1854

For the wages of sin is death; but the gift of God is eternal life through Jesus Christ our Lord. —Romans 6:23—KJV

For the wages of sin is death, but the gift of God is eternal life in Christ Jesus our Lord. —Romans 6:23—NIV

In this verse, the death that is spoken of is the wages or consequence of sin. This death is due to the penal sanction of God's law. In presenting the subject of our text, I must illustrate the nature of sin, specify some of the attributes of the penal sanctions of God's law, and show what this penalty must be.

The nature of sin.

An illustration will give us the best practical view of the nature of sin. Suppose a government established to secure the highest well-being of the governed and of the ruling authorities. Suppose the head of this government used all of his attributes in this enterprise—all of his wealth, time, and energy—in order to achieve the worthy goal of the highest general good. For this purpose, he enacts the best possible laws—laws which, if obeyed, will secure the highest good of both subject and Prince. He then takes care to affix adequate penalties; otherwise, all his care and wisdom would come to nothing. He devotes to the interests of his government all he is and all he has without reserve or abatement.

Now, suppose some of his subjects refuse to sympathize with this movement. They say, "charity begins at home," and they are for taking care of themselves first. In short, they are thoroughly selfish. It is easy to see what this would be in a human government. The man who does this becomes the common enemy of the government and of all its subjects. This is sin. This illustrates precisely the case of the sinner. Sin is selfishness. Sin sets up a selfish end or goal, and to gain it, sin uses selfish means. In respect to both its end and means, sin opposes God and all the goals of general happiness that He seeks to secure. Sin denies God's rights and discards God's interests. Each sinner maintains that his own will shall be the law. The interest he sets himself to secure is entirely opposed to the interests proposed by God in His government.

All law must have sanctions.

Without sanctions or consequences, law would be only advice. It is therefore essential to the distinctive and inherent nature of law that the law has sanctions. Sanctions are either remuneratory or vindicatory. They promise reward for obedience (are remuneratory), and they threaten penalty for disobedience (are vindicatory). They are vindicatory inasmuch as they vindicate the honor of the violated law.

Sanctions may be either natural or governmental. Often both forms exist in other governments than the divine. Natural penalties are those evil consequences that naturally result without any direct interference of government to punish. Thus in all governments, the disrespect of its friends falls as a natural penalty on transgressors. They are the natural enemies of all good subjects. In the divine government, compunctions of conscience and remorse fall into this class of natural penalties, and indeed many other things that naturally result from obedience and disobedience. There should also be governmental sanctions. Every governor should manifest his displeasure against the violation of his laws. To leave the whole question of obedience to mere natural consequences is obviously not just to society. Inasmuch as governments are established to uphold the law and secure obedience, they are bound to put forth their utmost energies in this work.

Another incidental agency of government under some circumstances is what we call discipline. One object of discipline is to go before the infliction of the penalty to force open unwilling eyes so they will see that the law has a government to back it up and the sinner has a fearful penalty to fear. During their probation, people can suffer discipline before they have seen or felt the fearfulness of the penalty. The design of discipline is to admonish them—to make them think and consider. Thus, the special object of discipline is the good of the subject on whom it falls and of those who may witness its administration. Discipline does not propose to sustain the dignity of the law by exemplary inflictions, which belong exclusively to the province of penalty. Discipline, therefore, is not penal in the sense of visiting crime with deserved punishment, but aims to dissuade the subject of law from violating its precepts.

Disciplinary agency could scarcely exist under a government of pure law, for the reason that such a government cannot defer the infliction of penalty. Discipline presupposes a state of suspended penalty. Hence, penal inflictions must be broadly distinguished from disciplinary.

We are sinners, therefore, we have little occasion to dwell on the remuneratory features of God's government. We can have no claim to remuneration under the law. Remuneration under the law is precluded utterly by our sin. However, with the penal features we have everything to do.

Attributes of the penal sanctions of God's law.

God has given us reason. This affirms intuitively and irresistibly all the great truths of moral government. There are certain attributes that we know must belong to the moral law; one is, intrinsic justice. Penalty

12

Romans 6:23

should threaten no more and no less than is just. Justice must be an attribute of God's law; or else the whole universe must inevitably condemn it.

Intrinsic justice means and implies that the penalty be equal to the obligation violated. The guilt of sin consists in its being a violation of obligation. Hence, the guilt must be in proportion to the magnitude of the obligation violated, and consequently the penalty must be measured by this obligation.

Governmental justice is another attribute. This feature of law seeks to afford security against transgression. Law is not governmentally just unless its penalty is graduated to afford the highest security against sin that the nature of the case admits. Suppose under any government the sanctions of law are trifling and not at all proportioned to the end to be secured. Such a government is unjust to itself and to the interests it is committed to maintain. Hence, a good government must be governmentally just, affording in the severity of its penalties and the certainty of their just infliction the highest security that its law shall be obeyed.

Penal sanctions should be worthy of the goal aimed at by the law and by its author. Government is only a means to an end—this proposed end being universal obedience and its consequent happiness. If law is indispensable for obtaining this end, its penalty should be graduated accordingly. Hence, the penalty should be graduated by the importance of the precept. If the precept is of fundamental importance—of such importance that disobedience to it saps the very existence of all government—then it should be guarded by the greatest and most solemn sanctions. The penalties attached to its violation should be of the highest order.

Penalty should make an adequate expression of the lawgiver's views of the value of the purpose he proposes to secure by law; also of his views of the sacredness of his law; also of the intrinsic guilt of disobedience. Penalty aims to show forth the heart of the lawgiver—to show the earnestness of his desire to maintain the right and to secure that order and well-being which depend on obedience. In the greatness of the penalty, the lawgiver brings forth his heart and pours the whole influence of his character upon his subjects.

The object of executing the penalty is precisely the same; not to gratify revenge, as some seem to suppose, but to act on the subjects of government with influences toward obedience. It has the same general object the law itself has. Penal sanctions should be an adequate expression of the lawgiver's regard for the public good and of his interest in it. In the precept he gives some expression; in the penalty, he gives yet more. In the precept, we see the object in view and have a manifestation of regard for the public interests. In the penalty, we have a measure of this regard, showing us how great it is.

Consider this example, suppose a human law were to punish murder with only a trifling penalty. Under the pretense of being very tenderhearted, suppose the lawgiver decided the crime of murder should have a penalty of a fine of fifty cents! Would this penalty show that he greatly loved his subjects and highly valued their life and interests? Far from it! You cannot feel that a legislator has done his duty unless he shows how much he values human life, and unless he attaches a penalty commensurate in some good degree with the end to be secured.

One word needs to be said regarding the infliction of capital punishment in human governments. There is a difference of opinion as to which is most effective, solitary punishment for life or death. Leaving this question without remark, I have it to say that no one ever doubts that the murderer deserves to die. If some other punishment than death is to be preferred, it is not by any means because the murderer does not deserve death. No one can doubt this for a moment. It is one of the unalterable principles of righteousness that if a man sacrifices the interest of another, he sacrifices his own; an eye for an eye; life for life. We cannot but affirm that no government lays sufficient stress on the protection of human life unless it guards this trust with its highest penalties. Where life and all its vital interests are at stake, there the penalty should be great and solemn as is possible.

Moral agents have two sides to their sensibility or feeling—hope and fear—to which you may address the prospect of good and the dread of evil. I am now speaking of penalty. Penalty is addressed only to fear.

I have said in substance that penalty should adequately assert and vindicate the rightful authority of the lawgiver; should afford if possible an adequate rebuke of sin and should be based on a just appreciation of its

12

Romans 6:23

nature. God's moral government embraces the entire intelligent universe, and stretches with its vast results onward through eternity. Hence, the sweep and breadth of its interests are absolutely unlimited, and consequently the penalties of its law, being set to vindicate the authority of this government and to sustain these immeasurable interests, should be beyond measure dreadful. If anything beyond and more dreadful than the threatened penalty could be conceived, all minds would say, "This is not enough." With any just views of the relations and the guilt of sin, they could not be satisfied unless the penalty is the greatest that is conceivable. Sin is so vile, so mischievous, so terribly destructive and so far sweeping in its ruin, moral agents could not feel that enough is done so long as more can be done.

We now need to discuss the penalty of God's moral law. Our text says that the penalty is death. This certainly is not animal death, for saints and animals die, neither of whom can be receiving the wages of sin. Besides, this would be no penalty if, after its infliction, people went at once to heaven. Such a penalty, considered as the wages of sin, would only be an insult to God's government.

Furthermore, this death cannot be spiritual death, for spiritual death is nothing else than a state of entire disobedience to the law. You cannot well conceive of anything more absurd than to punish a person for disobedience by subjecting him to perpetual disobedience—an effort to sustain the law by dooming such offenders to its perpetual violation and nothing more.

The death that Paul writes of in this verse is endless misery, corresponding to the death penalty in human governments. Everybody knows what this is. It separates the criminal from society forever; debars him at once and utterly from all the privileges of the government and consigns him over to hopeless ruin. Nothing more dreadful can be inflicted. It is the extreme penalty, fearful beyond any other that is possible for human beings to inflict. There can be no doubt that death as spoken of in our text is intended to correspond to the death penalty in human governments.

You will also observe that in our text the "gift of God" which is "eternal life through Jesus Christ our Lord" is directly contrasted with death, the wages of sin. This fact may throw light on the question respecting the nature of this death. We must look for the antithesis of "eternal life." Eternal life is not merely an eternal existence. In the scriptures, eternal life never means merely an eternal existence. Eternal life means a state of eternal blessedness, implying eternal holiness as its foundation. The use of the term "life" in scripture in the sense of real life—a life worth living—real and rich enjoyment, is so common as to supersede the necessity of special proof. The penalty of death is therefore the opposite of this—eternal misery.

Objections raised against the doctrine of eternal punishment.

All of the objections I have ever heard amount only to this, that eternal punishment is unjust. They may be expressed in somewhat various phraseology, but this is the only idea that they involve of any moment at all.

Eternal punishment is claimed to be unjust because "life is so short." How strangely people talk! Life is so short that people do not have time to sin enough to deserve eternal death! Do people forget that one sin incurs the penalty due for sinning? How many sins ought it to take to make one transgression of the law of God? People often talk as if they supposed it must require a great many. As if a person must commit a great many murders before he has made up the crime of murder enough to fall under the sentence of the court! What! Shall a person come before the court and plead that although he has broken the law to be sure, yet he has not lived long enough and broken the law enough times to incur its penalty? What court on earth ever recognized such a plea as proving any other than the folly and guilt of him who made it?

Some urge that "man is so small, so very insignificant a being that he cannot possibly commit an infinite sin." What does this objection mean? Does it mean that sin is an act of creation, and to be measured therefore by the magnitude of that something which it creates? This would be an exceedingly wild idea of the nature of sin. Does the objection mean that people cannot violate an obligation of infinite strength? Then his meaning is simply false, as everybody must know. Does he imply that the guilt of sin is not to be measured by the obligation violated? Then he

12

Romans 6:23

knows not what he says, or wickedly denies known truth. What! People are so little that they cannot commit much sin! Is this the way we reason in analogous cases? Suppose your child disobeys you. He is very much smaller than you are! Do you therefore exonerate him from blame? Is this a reason which nullifies his guilt? Can no sin be committed by inferiors against their superior? Have sensible people always been mistaken in supposing that the younger and smaller are sometimes under obligations to obey the older and the greater? Suppose you smite down the magistrate. Suppose you insult or attempt to assassinate the king. Are these very small crimes, almost too excusable to be deemed a crime at all because you are in a lower position and they are in a higher? You say, "I am so little, so very insignificant! How can I deserve so great a punishment?" Do you reason so in any other case except your own sins against God? Never!

Some say, "Sin is not an infinite evil." This language is ambiguous. Does it mean that sin would not work infinite mischief if suffered to run on indefinitely? This is false, for if only one soul were ruined by it, the mischief accruing from it would be infinite. Does it mean that sin is not an infinite evil as seen in its present results and relations? Suppose this is admitted; it proves nothing to our purpose, for it may be true that the sum total of evil results from each single sin will not all be brought out in any duration less than eternity. How then can you measure the evil of sin by what you see today?

But there are still other considerations to show that the penalty of the law must be infinite. Sin is an infinite natural evil. It is so in this sense, that there are no bounds to the natural evil it would introduce if not governmentally restrained. If sin were to ruin but one soul, there could be no limit set to the evil it would thus occasion.

Sin involves infinite guilt, for it is a violation of infinite obligation. Here it is important to notice a common mistake growing out of the confusion of ideas about the ground of obligation. From this confusion results mistakes with regard to what constitutes the guilt of sin. Here I might show that when you misapprehend the ground of obligation, you will almost of necessity misconceive the nature and extent of sin and guilt. Let us recur to our former illustration. Here is a government wisely framed to secure the highest good of the governed and of all concerned. Whence arises the obligation to obey? Certainly from the intrinsic value of the end sought to be secured. But how broad is this obligation to obey; or in other words, what is its true measure? I answer, it exactly equals the value of the end which the government seeks to secure, and which obedience will secure, but which sin will destroy. By this measure, the penalty must be graduated. By this the lawgiver must determine how much sanction, remuneratory and vindicatory, he must attach to his law in order to meet the demands of justice and benevolence.

God's law aims to secure the highest universal good. Its chief and ultimate end is not, strictly speaking, to secure supreme homage to God, but rather to secure the highest good of all intelligent moral beings—God and all His creatures. So viewed, you will see that the intrinsic value of the end to be sought is the real ground of obligation to obey the precept. The value of this end being estimated, you have the value and strength of the obligation.

This is plainly infinite in the sense of being unlimited. In this sense we affirm obligation to be without limit. The very reason why we affirm any obligation at all is that the law is good and is the necessary means of the highest good of the universe. Hence the reason why we affirm any penalty at all compels us to affirm the justice and necessity of an infinite penalty. We see that intrinsic justice must demand an infinite penalty for the same reason that it demands any penalty whatever. If any penalty be just, it is just because law secures a certain good. If this good aimed at by the law be unlimited in extent, so must be the penalty. Governmental justice thus requires endless punishment; else it provides no sufficient guaranty for the public good.

The law not only designs but tends to secure infinite good. Its tendencies are directed to this end. Hence, its penalty should be infinite. The law is not just to the interests it both aims and tends to secure unless it arms itself with infinite sanctions. Nothing less than infinite penalty can be an adequate expression of God's view of the value of the great end on which His heart is set. When people talk about eternal death being too great a penalty for sin, what do they think of God's efforts to restrain sin all over the moral universe? What do they think of the death of His well-beloved Son? Do they suppose it possible that God could give an adequate, or a

12

corresponding expression to His hatred of sin by any penalty less than endless? Nothing less could give an adequate expression to His regard for the authority of law. O, how fearful the results and how shocking the very idea, if God should fail to make an adequate expression of His regard for the sacredness of that law which underlies the entire weal of all His vast kingdom! You would insist that He shall regard the violation of His law as Universalists do! How surely He would bring down an avalanche of ruin on all His intelligent creatures if He were to yield to your demands! Were He to affix anything less than endless penalty to His law, what holy being could trust the administration of His government!

His regard to the public good forbids His attaching a light or finite penalty to His law. He loves His subjects too well. Some people have strange notions of the way in which a ruler should express his regard for his subjects. They would have him so tenderhearted toward the guilty that they should absorb his entire sympathy and regard. They would allow him perhaps to fix a penalty of six pence fine for the crime of murder, but not much if anything more. The poor murderer's wife and children are so precious you must not take away much of his money, and as to touching his liberty or his life—neither of these is to be thought of. What! Do you not know that human nature is very frail and temptable, and therefore you ought to deal very sparingly with penalties for murder? Perhaps they would say, you may punish the murderer by keeping him awake one night—just one, no more; and God may let a guilty man's conscience disturb him about to this extent for the crime of murder! Universalists tell us that they will allow the Most High God to give a person a conscience that shall trouble him a little if he commits murder—a little, say for the first and perhaps the second offence; but they are not wont to notice the fact that under this penalty of a troubling conscience, the more a person sins, the less he has to suffer. Under the operation of this descending scale, it will soon come to this, that a murderer would not get so much penalty as the loss of one night's sleep. But such are the notions that people reach when they swing clear of the affirmations of an upright reason and of God's revealing word.

Speaking now to those who have a moral sense to affirm the right as well as eyes to see the operation of law, I know you cannot deny the logical necessity of the death-penalty for the moral law of God. There is a logical clinch to every one of these propositions which you cannot escape.

No penalty less than infinite and endless can be an adequate expression of God's displeasure against sin and of His determination to resist and punish it. The penalty should run on as long as there are subjects to be affected by it—as long as there is need of any demonstration of God's feelings and governmental course toward sin. God certainly can inflict an endless and infinite punishment. If, therefore, the exigency demands the greatest penalty He can inflict, this must be the penalty—banishment from God and endless death.

The gospel everywhere assumes the same. It holds that by the deeds of the law no flesh can be justified before God. Indeed, it not only affirms this, but builds its entire system of atonement and grace upon this foundation. It constantly assumes that there is no such thing as paying the debt and canceling obligation; therefore, the sinner's only relief is forgiveness through redeeming blood.

Yet again, if the penalty be not endless death, what is it? Is it temporary suffering? Then how long does it last? When does it end? Has any sinner ever got through; served out his time and been taken to heaven? We have no testimony to prove such a case, not one; but we have the solemn testimony of Jesus Christ to prove that there never can be such a case. He tells us that there can be no passing from hell to heaven or from heaven to hell. A great gulf is fixed between over which none shall ever pass. You may pass from earth to heaven, or from earth to hell; but these two states of the future world are wide extremes, and no man or angel shall pass the gulf that divides them.

Suppose you answer my question, "What is the penalty?" And you make the reply, "It is only the natural consequences of sin as developed in a troubled conscience." Then it follows that the more a man sins the less he is punished, until it amounts to an infinitesimal quantity of punishment, for which the sinner cares just nothing at all. Who can believe this? Under this system, if a man fears punishment, he has only to pitch into sinning with the more will and energy. He will have the comfort of feeling that he can very soon get over all his compunctions, and get beyond any penalty whatever! And do you believe this is God's only punishment

12

Romans 6:23

for sin? You cannot believe it.

Universalists always confound discipline with penal sanctions. They overlook this fundamental distinction and regard all that people suffer here in this world as only penal. Whereas it is scarcely penal at all, but is chiefly disciplinary. They ask, "What good will it do a sinner to send him to an endless hell? Is not God perfectly benevolent, and if so, how can He have any other object than to do the sinner all the good he can?" I reply that punishment is not designed to do good to that sinner who is punished. It looks to other, remoter, and far greater good. Discipline, while he was on earth, sought mainly his personal good; penalty looks to other results. If you ask, "Does not God aim to do good to the universal public by penalty?" I answer, "Even so; that is precisely what He aims to do."

Under human governments, the penalty may aim in part to reclaim. So far, it is discipline. But the death-penalty—after all suspension is past, and the fatal blow comes, aims not to reclaim, and is not discipline but is only penalty. The guilty man is laid on the great public altar and made a sacrifice for the public good. The object is to make a fearful, terrible impression on the public mind of the evil of transgression and the fearfulness of its consequences. Discipline looks not so much to the support of law as to the recovery of the offender. But the day of judgment has nothing to do with reclaiming the lost sinner. That and all its issues are purely penal. It is strange that these obvious facts should be overlooked.

Underlying any safe dispensation of discipline there must be a moral law sustained by ample and fearful sanctions to preserve the law-giver's authority and sustain the majesty and honor of his government. It would not be safe to trust a system of discipline (and it could not be expected to take hold of the ruined with much force), if it were not sustained by a system of law and penalty. The penal visitation on the unreclaimed sinner must stand forever, an appalling fact, to show that justice is realized, law vindicated, God honored, and to make an enduring and awful impression of the evil of sin and of God's eternal hostility against it.

REMARKS

We hear a great many cavils against future punishment. At these we should not so much wonder, but for the fact that the gospel assumes this truth, and then proposes a remedy. One would naturally suppose the mind would shrink from those fearful conclusions to which it is pressed when the relations of mere laws are contemplated; but when the gospel interposes to save, then it becomes passing strange that people should admit the reality of the gospel, and yet reject the law and its penalties. They talk of grace; but what do they mean by grace? When people deny the fact of sin, there is no room and no occasion for grace in the gospel. Admitting nominally the fact of sin, but virtually denying its guilt, grace is only a name. Repudiating the sanctions of the law of God and laboring to disprove their reality, what right have people to claim that they respect the gospel? They make it only a farce—or at least a system of amends for unreasonably severe legislation under the legal economy. Let no one who so traduces the law assume that they honor God by applauding His gospel!

The representations of the Bible with regard to the final doom of the wicked are exceedingly striking. Spiritual truths are revealed by natural objects: for example, the gates and walls of the New Jerusalem to present the splendors and glories of the heavenly state. A spiritual telescope is put into our hands. We are permitted to point it toward the glorious city "whose builder and Maker is God." We may survey its inner sanctuary, where the worshipping hosts praise God without ceasing. We see their flowing robes of white—the palms of victory in their hands—the beaming joy of their faces—the manifestations of ineffable bliss in their souls. This is heaven portrayed in symbol. Who supposes that this is intended as hyperbole? Who arraigns these representations as extravagant in speech, as if designed to overrate the case, or raise unwarrantable expectations? No one believes this. No one ever brings this charge against what the Bible says of heaven. What is the object in adopting this figurative mode of representation? Beyond question, the object is to give the best possible conception of the facts.

Then we have the other side. The veil is lifted, and you come to the very verge of hell to see what is there. Whereas on the one hand all was glorious, on the other all is fearful, and full of horrors.

There is a bottomless pit. A deathless soul is cast therein. It sinks and

12

Romans 6:23

sinks and sinks, going down that awful pit which knows no bottom, weeping and wailing as it descends, and you hear its groans as they echo and re-echo from the sides of that dread cavern of woe!

Here is another image. You have a "lake of fire and brimstone," and you see lost sinners thrown into its waves of rolling fire. They lash its burning shore and gnaw their tongues for pain. There the worm dieth not, and their fire is not quenched. Not one drop of water can reach them to "cool their tongues," "tormented in that flame."

What think you? Has God said these things to frighten our poor souls? Did He mean to play on our fears for His own amusement? Can you think so? Nay, does it not rather grieve His heart that He must build such a hell, and must plunge therein the sinners who will not honor His law—will not embrace salvation from sinning through His grace? Ah, the waves of death roll darkly under the eye of the Holy and compassionate One! He has no pleasure in the death of the sinner! But He must sustain His throne and save His loyal subjects if He can.

Turn to another scene. Here is a death-bed. Did you ever see a sinner die? Can you describe the scene? Was it a friend, a relative, dear, very dear to your heart? How long was he dying? Did it seem to you the death-agony would never end? When my last child died, the struggle was long; O, it was fearfully protracted and agonizing! Twenty-four hours in the agonies of dissolving nature! It made me sick; I could not see it! But suppose it had continued till this time. I should long since have died myself under the anguish and nervous exhaustion of witnessing such a scene. So would all our friends. Who could survive to the final termination of such an awful death? Who would not cry out, "My God, cut it short, cut it short in mercy!" When my wife died, her death-struggles were long and heart-rending. If you had been there, you would have cried mightily to God, "Cut it short! O, cut it short and relieve this dreadful agony!" But suppose it had continued, on and on, by day and by night—day after day, through its slow moving hours, and night after night—long nights, as if there could be no morning. The figure of our text supposes an eternal dying. Let us conceive such a case. Suppose it should actually occur in some dear circle of sympathizing friends. A poor man cannot die! He lingers in the death-agony a month, a year, five years, ten years—till all his friends are broken down and fall into their graves under the insupportable horror of the scene: but still the poor man cannot die! He outlives one generation; then another and another; one hundred years he is dying in mortal agony and yet he comes no nearer to the end! What would you think of such a scene? It would be an illustration—that is all—a feeble illustration of the awful "second death!"

God would have us understand what an awful thing sin is and what fearful punishment it deserves. He would fain show us by such figures how terrible must be the doom of the determined sinner. Did you ever see a sinner die? And did you not cry out, "Surely the curse of God has fallen heavily on this world!" Ah, this is only a faint emblem of that heavier curse that comes in the "second death!"

The text affirms that death is the "wages of sin." It is just what sin deserves. Laborers earn wages and create a rightful claim to such remuneration. So sinners are conceived as earning wages when they sin. They become entitled to their pay. God deems himself beholden to give them their well-deserved wages.

As I have often said, I would not say one word in this direction to distress your souls if there were no hope and no mercy possible. Would I torment you before the time? God forbid! Would I hold out the awful penalty before you, and tell you there is no hope? No. I say these things to make you feel the need of escaping for your life.

Think of this: "the wages of sin is death!" God is aiming to erect a monument that shall proclaim to all the universe—Stand in awe and sin not! So that whenever they shall look on this awful expression, they shall say, "What an awful thing sin is!" People are prone to exclaim, "O, how horrible the penalty!" They are but too apt to overlook the horrible guilt and ill-desert of sin! When God lays a sinner on his death-bed before our eyes, He invites us to look at the penalty of sin. There he lies, agonizing, groaning, quivering, racked with pain, yet he lives, and lives on. Suppose he lives on in this dying state a day, a week, a month, a year, a score of years, a century, a thousand years, a thousand ages, and still he lives on dying perpetually yet never dead. Finally, the universe passes away; the heavens are rolled together as a scroll, and what then? There lies that sufferer yet. He looks up and cries out, "How long, O HOW LONG?" Like the

12

Romans 6:23

knell of eternal death, the answer comes down to him, "Eternally, ETER-NALLY." Another cycle of eternal ages rolls on, and again he dares to ask, "How long?" Again the answer rolls back, "Eternally, ETERNALLY!" O how this fearful answer comes down thundering through all the realms of agony and despair

We are informed that in the final consummation of earthly scenes, the judgment shall sit and the books shall be opened. We shall be there, and what is more, there to close up our account with our Lord and receive our allotment. Which will you have on that final settlement day? The wages of sin? Do you say, "Give me my wages! Give me my wages! I will not be indebted to Christ?" Sinner, you shall have them. God will pay you without fail or stint. He has made all the necessary arrangements, and has your wages ready. But take care what you do! Look again before you take your final leap. Soon the curtain will fall, probation close, and all hope will have perished. Where then shall I be? And you, where? On the right hand or on the left?

The Bible locates hell in the sight of heaven. The smoke of their torment as it rises up forever and ever is in full view from the heights of the Heavenly City. There, you adore and worship; but as you cast your eye afar off toward where the rich man lay, you see what it costs to sin. There, not one drop of water can go to cool their burning tongues. Thence the smoke of their torment rises and rises for evermore. Take care what you do today!

Suppose you are looking into a vast crater, where the surges of molten lava boil and roll up, and roll and swell, and ever and anon belch forth huge masses to deluge the plains below. Once in my life, I stood in sight of Etna and looked down into its awful mouth. I could not forbear to cry out "Tremendous. TREMENDOUS!" "There," said I, "is an image of hell!" O, sinner, think of hell, and of yourself thrust into it. It pours forth its volumes of smoke and flame forever, never ceasing, never exhausted. Upon that spectacle the universe can look and read, "The wages of sin is death! O, sin not, since such is the doom of the unpardoned sinner!" Think what a demonstration this is in the government of God! What an exhibition of His holy justice, of His inflexible purpose to sustain the interests of holiness and happiness in all His vast dominions! Is not this worthy of God, and of the sacredness of His great scheme of moral government?

Sinner, you may now escape this fearful doom. This is the reason why God has revealed hell in His faithful word. And now shall this revelation, to you, be in vain and worse than in vain?

What would you think if this whole congregation were pressed by some resistless force close up to the very brink of hell: but just as it seemed that we are all to be pushed over the awful brink, an angel rushes in, shouting as with seraphic trump, "Salvation is possible! Glory to God, GLORY TO GOD, GLORY TO GOD!"

You cry aloud, "Is it possible?" "Yes, yes," he cries, "Let me take you up in my broad, loving arms, and bear you to the feet of Jesus, for He is mighty and willing to save!"

Is all this mere talk? O, if I could wet my lips with the dews of heaven, and bathe my tongue in its founts of eloquence, even then I could not describe the realities.

Christian people, are you figuring round and round to get a little property, yet neglecting souls? Beware, lest you ruin souls that can never live again! Do you say. "I thought they knew it all?" They reply to you, "I did not suppose you believed a word of it yourselves. You did not act as if you did. Are you going to heaven? Well, I am going down to hell! There is no help for me now. You will sometimes think of me then, as you shall see the smoke of my woe rising up darkly athwart the glorious heavens. After I have been there a long, long time, you will sometimes think that I, who once lived by your side, am there. O remember, you cannot pray for me then; but you will remember that once you might have warned and might have saved me."

O, I think, if there can be bitterness in heaven, it must enter through such an avenue and spoil your happiness there!

12

Romans 6:23

---

* Charles G. Finney, "The Oberlin Evangelist," July 5, 1854, *Sermons on Gospel Themes*, 37–56, *Principles of Victory*, 74–86. For Review: Answer the Study Questions on page 182, Cowles page 204.

Jesus on Righteousness

Jesus replied, "Let it be so now; it is proper for us to do this to fulfill all righteousness." Then John consented. —Matthew 3:15

Blessed are those who hunger and thirst for righteousness, for they will be filled. —Matthew 5:6

Blessed are those who are persecuted because of righteousness, for theirs is the kingdom of heaven. —Matthew 5:10

For I tell you that unless your righteousness surpasses that of the Pharisees and the teachers of the law, you will certainly not enter the kingdom of heaven. —Matthew 5:20

Be careful not to do your "acts of righteousness" before men, to be seen by them. If you do, you will have no reward from your Father in heaven. —Matthew 6:1

But seek first his kingdom and his righteousness, and all these things will be given to you as well. —Matthew 6:33

For John came to you to show you the way of righteousness, and you did not believe him, but the tax collectors and the prostitutes did. And even after you saw this, you did not repent and believe him. —Matthew 21:32

When he comes, he will convict the world of guilt in regard to sin and righteousness and judgment: in regard to sin, because men do not believe in me; in regard to righteousness, because I am going to the Father, where you can see me no longer; and in regard to judgment, because the prince of this world now stands condemned. —John 16:8-11

Study Questions
for Individuals and Groups

T he study questions in *Principles of Righteousness* will serve as a review and help you focus your thoughts on some of the main teachings in each of Charles Finney's sermons on Paul's Letter to the Romans. You can use these questions for personal enrichment and for small group study. Experience indicates that probably no more than five questions can be discussed fully in one hour, so you may want to omit some questions or hold a longer discussion. The study questions that are obviously phrased for a group discussion can be thought about individually. You can also find these questions formatted as helpful handouts for groups or as study guides for notebooks, along with other helpful materials, at the Finney's Principles website at FinneysPrinciples.org. Some may also choose to discuss these and other questions online with people around the world. For online discussion, the editor recommends the Finney-works Group, which can be found at groups.yahoo.com, or visit FinneysPrinciples.org for more information.

1. The Wrath of God Against Those Who Withstand His Truth

1. In this lesson, what did you learn that was new to you? Did you find anything in this lesson that relates to your own life? What aspects of your own life do you need to change in order to avoid withstanding the truth of God? List three things in your life that you want to change.

2. Define these terms: sin, ungodliness, unrighteousness, and wickedness. Today, how comfortable are people when they hear these terms used in describing behavior, especially their behavior? How can Christians help people face the consequences of their behavior so they will repent and place their faith in Jesus Christ as Lord and Savior?

3. Since truth is a natural stimulus to the mind, how can knowing this fact assist and encourage you in your work of evangelism?

4. How does Finney describe the workings of our conscience? Define "a sense of obligation."

5. Why do you agree or disagree with this statement: "The very apprehending of moral truth concerning God renders it impossible to be indifferent" (see page 4)? Can you confirm or refute Finney's belief by considering how Peter and John, Ananias and Sapphira, and the high priest and council responded to the gospel of Jesus Christ (see Acts 2-7)?

6. What is the difference between legal obligation and moral obligation? How does refusing to live in accordance with either impact both church and society?

7. Describe the difference between moral honesty and moral dishonesty. How can misunderstanding the Christian faith lead some to remain morally dishonest?

8. List and discuss three ways that God reveals His wrath. Can you think of other ways that Finney omitted in this particular sermon?

9. What is a spurious convert? Discuss how spurious converts can act. How are they made? Would you consider Ananias and Sapphira spurious converts? If so, why? Are spurious converts still a problem today in churches? How can this problem be solved today?

10. What can be done to change selfish "Christians" and what should they be changed into? What can be done to change a selfish "Church"?

2. *God's Wrath Against Those Who Withstand His Truth*

1. What do the terms "righteous" and "unrighteous" mean?

2. How would you describe in more detail "benevolent displeasure"? Can you think of a better way to describe "the wrath of God"? Why do you think some churches (preachers) avoid talking about the wrath of God?

3. Compare Finney's exposition of how God reveals His wrath in this sermon and in the previous sermon. Does Finney offer any tender encouragement in either sermon; if so, how? How can you offer this?

4. What is the difference between "ungodliness" and "unrighteousness," if any? Do you agree or disagree with Finney's definitions? Why?

5. What can discerning the shortcomings of others indicate about the critic and the critic's obedience? How can this be a problem?

6, What does "holding back the truth" imply about the sinner? Do you agree that sinners do this? How would you talk to a sinner about this?

7. What arguments seem the best regarding ability or inability to obey God? Do average people seem concerned about this debate today?

8. What would you think of God if He did not express His indignation against sinning? How can you use this idea to help lead a sinner to repentance and faith?

9. Why is it not "mean of God" to send sinners to hell? How can you convince people today that hell exists and is necessary after this life?

10. In this sermon, how effective do you think it was for Finney to share his dream? Do you think his approach to dreams is wise or too narrow? What is the reason for your answer?

3. Holding the Truth in Unrighteousness

1. Do you think Finney improved his sermons on this text each time he preached them? Is there anything particular that you liked or disliked about any of these three sermons?

2. Why do you think Finney strongly emphasizes the "omission of duty" rather than the "commission of sin"? Was this wise or unwise?

3. How does Finney describe the "Freedom of the Will"? Do you agree or disagree with his description? If you disagree, how do you disagree?

4. Why does Finney emphasize "selfishness" in these sermons? How would you show a selfish person that they are selfish and that selfishness is wrong? Is "self-centered" a better term to use today? Why or why not?

5. Do you think this sermon could bring a revival to a church today as it did in Finney's day? Why or why not? How effective is preaching about neglect of duty to church members, especially when there are many other churches in a city or town they can attend if they want to feel good?

6. Do you agree or disagree that "stopping short of" or being unconcerned about sanctification can place a believer under the wrath of God? Why or why not? How would some people today argue against Finney's view? Can you think of a better way to teach on this topic?

7. What does the Law of God require? How does this relate to negative religion and positive religion?

8. Compare how the Law of God exhibits God and how the Gospel of God exhibits God. Why it is wise to exhibit God using both the Law of God and the Gospel of God?

9. Define "Disinterested Benevolence" in God and in the saint? What is a contemporary way of expressing this idea to sinners and saints?

10. Describe and distinguish what faith produces that the Law of God does not produce in a person and also in a church.

6. *The Foundation, Conditions, Relations and Results of Faith*

1. On what did Abraham's faith rest? Why do you think this is important, sufficient, or wrong? On what should faith rest today?

2. On what ground or foundation did God choose to justify sinners?

3. Name and describe three conditions of faith that Finney mentions in this sermon. Can you think of some conditions he did not mention?

4. Describe being treated in this life as governmentally righteous and as providentially a sinner. Do you think this is an accurate description of the situation of a pardoned sinner? Why or why not?

5. Why does faith naturally lead to obedience, joy, and peace?

6. What can a Christian do when he feels discouraged or distressed about his life and the various trials he is facing?

7. How can our faith overcome the flesh and Satan?

8. Distinguish among these theological concepts: the ground of faith, the conditions of faith, and faith itself.

9. How can obsessive self-examination lead away from faith in God?

10. How does Finney describe a weak faith, a loss of faith, or an unhealthy religion? How would you apply his teaching today?

7. The Rationality of Faith

1. How does Finney elaborate further on the meaning of faith in this sermon (especially distinguish between generic and specific forms of faith)? How do most define faith today?

2. What is the greatest trial to you faith? Why is this so? What is the greatest trial to faith for many in our world today?

3. What would you say to someone who stated, "I will not believe what I cannot understand"? And to someone who said, "You must first believe in order to understand"?

4. Why do you think Finney lists so many obstacles to belief in this sermon? Do you think this is helpful to believers or to nonbelievers? Why?

5. How can God's promises be an obstacle to faith? What promises of God present the greatest obstacles to faith today?

6. How does Finney show that people must live by faith in both the material and the spiritual realms? Is this helpful when discussing the Christian faith with nonbelievers?

7. How does Finney deal with the problem of sin and evil continuing to exist in our world?

8. How does belief that God has a good reason for the things that happen differ from the belief that God is in control of all that happens?

9. Describe how the law of progression works and how that law can be applied to the Bible and to the believer's study and practice of the Bible's teachings.

10. Why and how does Finney teach that we will continue to live by faith throughout eternity? Do you agree? Why or why not?

8. God's Love Commended to Us

1. How does God recommend His love to us? Why did God think this was necessary?

2. Why must we take God's love for us personally, as individuals? How does this relate to the General Atonement and the Limited Atonement?

3. How does God show that His love is unselfish?

4. Explain how God made it safe to pardon sinners. What does "pardon" mean? Why do we hear so little about "the pardon of sinners" today?

5. How does God show His abhorrence of sin? Explain. Why is this necessary? What are some examples of God showing His abhorrence today?

6. How does God teach us true love and enable us to love?

7. What is slavish fear? How does God's love subdue slavish fear? Why should He want to do this?

8. Why does the selfish sinner find it hard to pray?

9. Describe the difference between serving God in bondage and in liberty. How does the believer find this liberty?

10. Describe "saving faith." How does saving faith motivate the Christian? How does this differ from the notion of saving faith some have?

9. The Nature of Death to Sin

1. What is the difference between being "dead in sin" and "dead to sin"?

2. What does Finney mean by "a state of the will" in contrast to single volitions? How does this state affect and effect our choices?

3. When selfish reasons to take an action are presented to a person who is dead to sin, how will he usually respond? What is usually the controlling motive of his conduct?

4. How do you make decisions when you do not know what the will of God is in the situation?

5. What are the characteristics of a self-indulgent state of mind and a self-denying state of mind? Should Christians be concerned about these?

6. How does Finney compare death to sin with the process of physically dying on a deathbed? How could you improve Finney's comparison for both believers and unbelievers today?

7. What does it mean for "death to sin" to be "a state of mind"? Is "death in sin" also "a state of mind"? Explain your answer. Why does "making resolutions" not lead to "death to sin"?

8. Describe what Finney means by the baptism of the Holy Spirit, what this baptism achieves, and how we are to receive it. Do you agree or disagree with Finney's interpretation? Why or why not?

9. How does death to sin make our spiritual advancement more rapid? Is death to sin optional for a Christian and "saving faith"?

10. Why do people near physical death more easily enter into the state of "death to sin"? How can we and why should we enter into this state now, without waiting until we are near death?

10. Death to Sin through Christ

1. Describe what it means and how it feels to have sin as your Master.

2. What does it mean to be alive to God and dead to sin?

3. How does gospel salvation include being dead to sin?

4. What does the command or injunction to "reckon yourself wholly dead to sin" imply?

5. Why must I renounce all hope of attaining by my own unaided efforts and natural works this state of being dead to sin? What, then, can I do?

6. How does Finney compare becoming a Christian and taking marriage vows seriously? Do you think this is a good or helpful analogy to help keep Christians from sinning today? Why or why not?

7. How does Finney explain it when a Christian, in a state of being dead to sin, still sins sometimes? If he sins, does he lose his salvation?

8. Do you think it is reasonable to try to live without committing sins? Why or why not? How does this affect the church today?

9. What is the difference between being "convinced of sin" and being "convicted of sin"? Why does it seem more difficult to convict of sin today than in Finney's day?

10. How can you convince those who practice sin while professing to be good Christians that Jesus Christ came to save them from their sins, from sinning, and not just from the penalty of their sins?

11. Sanctification under Grace

1. What does Finney mean by saying sin is "a state of mind"? What state of mind is sin? Why is sin a voluntary state mind?

2. How does Finney contrast an "occasional temptation and sin" with "the dominion of sin as a state of mind"? Do you agree with this?

3. List three characteristics of living under or being under the law.

4. List three characteristics of living under or being under grace.

5. What are some benefits of being united with Christ?

6. Why does sin have dominion of a person who is under the law? Why can't the law help him or free him from the dominion of sin?

7. Describe the two predominant ways of interpreting the Seventh Chapter of Romans. What is Finney's view? What view do you agree with and why?

8. Why can't sin have dominion over a person who is under grace?

9. Do you agree or disagree with what Finney says it means to be a Christian? Why or why not? What do most today think it means to be a Christian? Do you agree or disagree? Why or why not? What can you say to help others believe as you do?

10. Distinguish between a legal reformation and regeneration (or true conversion)? How does it affect a church if most of the members have only experienced a legal reformation? How can this type of a church be changed?

12. The Wages of Sin

1. Why must governments have laws? Why must law have sanctions? What kinds of sanctions are there?

2. Describe natural and governmental sanctions. Why are both types of sanctions needed in God's government?

3. Distinguish between discipline and penalty in the wise exercise of government. Why are both needed? Are both in God's government? Why?

4. What can a penalty tell us about the lawgiver? What can the execution of a penalty tell us about a lawgiver?

5. Why does Finney say the wages of sin are eternal punishment instead of just physical death or spiritual death?

6. What is the aim, purpose, or ultimate end of God's law? How does this relate to our obligation to obey God's law?

7. Why is a guilty or troubled conscience an insufficient penalty for sin?

8. What is the Bible's purpose in the descriptions of both heaven and hell? What do these descriptions imply about God and His purpose in providing them for us?

9. How effective is Finney's comparing people dying (describing different deaths where he was a witness) with someone dying year after year, century after century, for eternity, as similar to eternal punishment? What effect should that have on his listeners/readers?

10. What hope does Finney give in this sermon? How does this hope help Finney preach as strongly as he does about eternal punishment?

If you have additional questions or comments to share with the editor or others, visit Finney's Principles website at FinneysPrinciples.org to contact L.G. Parkhurst, Jr. As soon as possible, we plan to publish the next book *Principles of Peace: Finney's Lessons on Romans*, Volume II. If you have comments or suggestions for this new book, please feel free to share them through FinneysPrinciples.org. We would also like to publish your testimonials about Finney's Principles at FinneysPrinciples.org.

Henry Cowles
Editor of the "Oberlin Evangelist"
1803-1881

Professor of Church History, Hebrew,

and Old Testament Literature

Henry Cowles
Commentary on Romans

Romans 1:16-20

Romans 1:16—*For I am not ashamed of the gospel of Christ for it is the power of God unto salvation to every one that believeth; to the Jew first, and also to the Greek.*

Paul would say with the strongest emphasis that his omission to visit Rome was by no means because he was ashamed of this gospel. He knew that Rome was a proud city, and the name of the crucified Nazarene of Galilee could not be popular and welcome there. Unmeasured reproach would naturally befall him were he to lift up that cross and name as his banner before the aristocracy and wealth and culture of that great city. However, never the first sense of shame should tinge his cheek or touch his sensibilities. Rather the gospel should be his highest glory, for in it there lay embodied and embosomed the glorious power of God unto the salvation of men, whether Jew or Gentile. Grandly does Paul assume that among all the interests and goods of earth there is nothing to be compared with the soul's salvation—the real saving of people from sin and

185

bringing them into the purity of truth and the unselfishness of love; into the blessed sympathies of heart-communion with the Infinite God. No work can be worthier and no labor more sublime than to be accumulating and wielding those forces which bring people out of their moral darkness into God's glorious light, lifting their lost souls out of moral ruin into God's great salvation. Therefore, Paul glories in the gospel of Christ, for God works in it and through it with His effective power toward and unto this salvation.

On this passage the reader's attention should be called particularly to the three following points: (1) That in and with this gospel there goes a power of God working unto the salvation of people, a power which is here and not elsewhere, which is so thoroughly involved in this gospel that Paul declares the gospel itself to be that power. This is a truth of surpassing interest and value. (2) That this power avails not to the salvation of all, but only of "every one that believeth." Paul might have left out this limitation if the truth in the case would have borne the omission, and doubtless he would. But, this limitation is a prime condition of the gospel as he held and taught it—salvation, not to all, but only to "every one that believeth." Paul knew very well that gospel truth, like all other truth, must be believed before it can have moral force on human souls. He will have some things to say soon about truth "held in unrighteousness"—held indeed, but *held down* and *held back* so that its moral power on the soul is worse than merely paralyzed. (3) This is the first pivotal text of the epistle. It propounds the first cardinal truth in the goodly system which this epistle will present and discuss.

Romans 1:17—*For therein is the righteousness of God revealed from faith to faith: as it is written, The just shall live by faith.*

This is the second pivotal passage of the epistle, holding in its nutshell form the grand truth of justification by faith as opposed to the Pharisaic scheme of justification by works of law. This passage, being thoroughly vital to the whole epistle and withal somewhat difficult by reason of its conciseness, should be carefully expounded.

I understand Paul to say that in the gospel God has revealed His mode of justifying sinners by and through their faith in Jesus Christ. Paul expresses this tersely in the words—"from faith to faith"—in the sense that it proceeds or comes from faith and it leads to the salvation of all people of faith—all true believers. This justification turns on faith as its condition; it requires faith and never can fail of being given to all who truly believe.

The make-up and shaping of this pregnant phrase—"from faith to faith"—seems to have sacrificed somewhat of clearness for the sake of brevity. Perhaps we may say that Paul sought a formula which should embody the grand central truth of the gospel system in the fewest possible words, making a phrase which might live in the memory, easily remembered, never forgotten.

We must take the words "to faith," not in their abstract sense, as to faith considered as a mental state or act, but in their concrete sense, as to the people of faith, those who truly believe. This is sufficiently clear from Paul's proof text out of Habakkuk 2.:4, where "the just" are certainly people in the concrete; just, good people, who have life before God through and by their faith. [[This seems to be the precise shade of meaning in the Greek words which Paul uses; for if he had meant precisely, the people justified by faith shall live, then the participle *dikaiomenos* rather than the adjective *dikaios* should have been his word.]] It is certain therefore that Paul was thinking of faith in Christ as leading to the salvation of the people of faith, real believers.

To go back for the moment to the standard phrase—"the righteousness of God"—we cannot take it in the sense of God's attribute of justice, abstractly considered; for the following reasons: (1) The word for that idea should have been *dikaioma* (as in Romans 1:32) and not as here *dikaiosune*. (2) The sense—abstract justice—does not correspond to the facts of the case; for it was not the particular mission of the gospel scheme to reveal the abstract justice of God, but rather His great mercy. (3) The gospel did purposely and most wonderfully reveal God's scheme for making sinful people righteous and accepted as such before Him. It reveals the great central fact that such justification comes through faith and avails unto all people of faith. (4) Finally, this exposition of the phrase—"the righteousness of God"—is fully sustained by Paul's subsequent use and explanation of it (see Romans 3:21-26; especially verses 21, 22)—"But now the righteousness of God without law is manifested, being witnessed by the law and the prophets; Even the righteousness of God which is by faith of Jesus Christ." This mode of justifying sinners is called God's mode—God's righteousness—for the good reason that it originated with God, not with man; is provided by God, not by man; emanating from God's wisdom and from His great love, and not from any, even the least, merit on the part of man.

In further defining this righteousness of God as being God's mode of making believers righteous before Him, it cannot be amiss to anticipate here what Paul will bring out very distinctly further on and say that it includes more than mere forgiveness of their sins, more than merely showing or declaring them to be accepted as righteous. The additional element—one of extremely vital value—is that of converting people from wickedness unto intrinsic righteousness of heart and life. God does not declare and show them to be righteous until they are radically and fundamentally transformed unto righteousness. Regeneration and repentance are thoroughly involved in this system as preliminary conditions, without which there can be no gospel justification. In Romans, chapters 6-8, Paul will elaborate these elements of the gospel scheme very thoroughly.

Romans 1:18—*For the wrath of God is revealed from heaven against all ungodliness and unrighteousness of men, who hold the truth in unrighteousness.*

It is entirely obvious that verse 18 is closely correlated to verse 17, using the same staple words. "The righteousness of God is revealed" opens verse 17. "The wrath of God is revealed" leads the thought in verse 18. But noticeably, the former—God's mode of making people righteous—is said to be revealed in the gospel ("therein"); but the wrath of God is not said to be revealed particularly in the gospel. Rather, Paul says that God's wrath is revealed "from heaven." He does not arrest his course of thought to describe to us the various or the special modes in which God makes this revelation, although some of its manifestations are referred to in Romans 1: 25, 26, and 28, which speak of God's righteously giving people up to self-reprobation so that their sin works out its natural results of more and more deep depravity, debasement and crime.

Let the reader be careful to note that the gospel scheme does and forever must assume God's deep, eternal displeasure against sin. Jesus came not to call the righteous but sinners to repentance. God's wrath is no causeless passion, no selfish irritation, no effervescence of hate. It is only the deep abhorrence of a holy soul against wrong; the irrepressible displeasure which infinite benevolence must feel toward all ungodliness and unrighteousness. Because God's character is so positively and intensely good, it is simply a necessity of His moral nature that He should dislike, loathe, condemn, all that is ungodly, unlike His own loving spirit; all that is unrighteous; that is to say, which recklessly tramples on the rights of others equally valuable as its own.

To misconstrue and pervert what the scriptures say of God's "wrath against sin" is unpardonably abusive to God and fearfully perilous to souls. Hence these few words of explanation are in place for the double purpose of truth and light to those who will receive it, and of solemn warning to those who despise it.

Those who practice ungodliness, against whom God's wrath is revealed from heaven, are further described here as "holding the truth in unrighteousness." In closely defining this phrase, we must choose between two somewhat different senses of the verb, "hold"—(1) Holding and continuing to hold the truth, yet in and with the practice of unrighteousness; living still in sin in spite of their knowledge of God's truth: or (2) Holding down, suppressing the truth, by resisting its claims because of their unrighteousness.

The latter understanding is to be preferred as most surely the real sense of Paul's word—(1) Because this verb means, not merely holding but holding down. But (2) and especially, because the entire drift of the subsequent context goes to develop this very process of holding down the truth, resisting its demands; "changing the truth of God into a lie;" not "glorifying God as God and not being thankful;" not "loving to retain God in their knowledge." Hence, it becomes very certain that Paul did not think of wicked people as continuing to hold the truth of God in the midst of their sinning; but rather, as suppressing, perverting, and changing it to a lie, and thus almost utterly paralyzing its legitimate moral power upon their heart. This will appear very clearly as we proceed.

Romans 1:19—*Because that which may be known of God is manifest in them; for God hath showed it unto them.*

In verse 18, Paul had assumed that wicked people have some real knowledge of God which in their wickedness they pervert and suppress. This being a thoroughly vital point, he here confirms that assumption.

His language is very expressive, but not easily translated into fully equivalent English words. It may be put thus: Because the knowable character of God—that in God which is knowable to mortals—is plain to them, for God has made it plain. This means that certain of the great and most vital elements in God's being and character are made plain to people by God's purposed revelation of himself. Paul proceeds to explain what people do know of God and how people abuse this knowledge and totally withstand the influence it should legitimately have upon their souls.

Romans 1:20—*For the invisible things of him from the creation of the world are clearly seen, being understood by the things that are made, even his eternal power and Godhead; so that they are without excuse:*

In brief paraphrase, thus—"For ever since the creation of the world, God's invisible attributes are distinctly seen, being apprehended by the human mind in His created works—these invisible attributes being His eternal power and Deity." This pregnant sentence, most compactly, tersely put, holds that God's otherwise invisible attributes have become in a sense visible to people ever since His creation of visible matter before their eyes; indeed, have become very distinctly visible, being mentally apprehended under the normal action of the human intelligence ("*nous*") in and by means of God's created works. Then Paul is careful to say that those invisible attributes of which he speaks are precisely God's eternal power and His Godhead, His real Deity. Beyond all question, God's works of creation manifest His boundless power and His truly divine attributes. None but God can create at all, giving existence where no existence was before; and yet more, none but God could create worlds of such vastness, majesty, beauty, glory. So, if people *do not* see God in these great works of His, it must be because they *will not*. Not to see God in these works is inexcusable guilt—as Paul proceeds to show.

On the sense of the word "from" in the clause—"from the creation of the world"—whether it be temporal [ever since in time], or logical ["from" as the source and fountain of knowledge], it would seem that both are involved, the temporal sense primarily; and then, as a consequence, the logical. That is, ever since the creation, those visible works have been an open manifestation of God's eternal power and Deity, in which, whoever would, might apprehend by his intelligence those great qualities of the Infinite Maker.*

---

*Cowles, Henry, *The Longer Epistles of Paul*, New York: D. Appleton & Company, 1880, pages 10-16.

Romans 3:20-28

Romans 3:20—*Therefore by the deeds of the law there shall no flesh be justified in his sight: for by the law is the knowledge of sin.*

The delicate point in this verse is the precise sense of its first word "Therefore" [Greek *dioti*] which some read *"therefore,"* making the impossibility of justification upon the basis of mere law an inference from what precedes in Romans 3:19; while others read it *"Because,"* introducing a new but collateral fact; which is, that no person can be justified by mere law, because the use and purpose of the law are to make sin more manifest—to give people a clearer, better knowledge of it. The former construction (that of the authorized version) is to be preferred, it being an undeniable inference from what precedes that no living person can be justified on the ground of perfect obedience to law, for he never obeys that law perfectly. The law has another use than that of becoming the ground of justification, which is, to give a more just view of sin, a *better knowledge of sin,* as Paul's word implies.

All this, the reader will notice, is preparing the way for the grand idea which Paul is about to introduce: God's new and perfect scheme for justifying sinners, through the gospel, by faith in the atoning Redeemer.

Romans 3:21—*But now the righteousness of God without the law is manifested, being witnessed by the law and the prophets;*
Romans 3:22—*Even the righteousness of God which is by faith of Jesus Christ unto all and upon all them that believe; for there is no difference:*
Romans 3:23—*For all have sinned, and come short of the glory of God:*

"But now"—"now" referring to the new light of the gospel scheme, set over against the dimness of the foregoing dispensation.—*Apart from law* (better than "without law"), on a scheme which does not lean upon law at all—God's plan of justifying people is made manifest—not indeed entirely new to people, for some testimony to it had been borne previously by the law and the prophets—the Old Testament Scriptures.

Even (verse 22) God's mode of justification "by faith of Jesus Christ" (by faith *in* Christ) availing unto all believing ones, for there is no difference between Jew and Gentile, all being equally under sin and equally precluded from salvation in any other possible way—all having sinned and having failed of the glorious approval of God—that glory which accrues from His final approbation and reward.

Romans 3: 24—*Being justified freely by his grace through the redemption that is in Christ Jesus:*
Romans 3: 25—*Whom God hath set forth to be a propitiation through faith in his blood, to declare his righteousness for the remission of sins that are past, through the forbearance of God:*
Romans 3: 26—*To declare, I say, at this time his righteousness: that he might be just, and the justifier of him which believeth in Jesus.*

These verses expand more fully God's wonderful scheme of justifying sinners by faith. "Being justified *gratuitously*"—as a free gift, not based at all upon their perfect obedience. "By his grace"—His real mercy, coming through that redemption which is provided for in Christ Jesus—

"Whom God has set forth, a propitiation," a propitiatory offering of a sacrificial nature, designed to make such atonement for sin as will render gratuitous pardon possible to God's mercy—made available to the sinner through faith in Christ's name. Then amplifying yet more the divine purpose in this propitiation, Paul adds, "For the purpose of showing his [God's] righteousness in the case of his remitting sins long past—the sins of the ages before Christ came which in God's great forbearance had been passed over—for the purpose of setting forth in this present time how He could be righteous in such remission—to show himself to be just and yet the justifier of him who has faith in Jesus. The two related things to be shown; that God is just to himself, just toward His law, His throne and all its interests, on the one hand; and on the other, the justifier of every believing one, accepting him as pardoned and justified on the ground of his faith in Christ—these together disclose the essence and explain the deep philosophy of this divine scheme of God for justifying sinners.

Reviewing this pregnant passage for the purpose of bringing out, if possible, yet more distinctly its salient and vital points, let it be noted:

1. That all along the foregoing ages God had been remitting the sins of His people.

2. But God had not shown clearly on what ground He had done this, nor how He could do it and yet be just to the interests of His moral government, just to His veracity in His threatenings against sin and sinners, and just to His responsibilities for the wellbeing of a universe of moral agents.

3. Something had indeed been done during the past ages toward illustrating the principles on which this remission of sin had taken place, particularly in the way of setting them forth under symbols and types which might at least serve to define a class of terms for future use, and so provide for a more clear manifestation of the vital things, at some future day.

4. Yet it still remained to make this final and far more lucid showing which should set forth *how* God could be just while yet He justified the believer in Jesus. The reader cannot fail to notice the great emphasis put by constant reiteration upon the idea of *setting forth, showing, making manifest*; nor can he fail to see that the thing to be made manifest was precisely what he puts in the phrase, "The righteousness of God by faith,"

and which he expands yet more as the showing how God could be at the same time *just* and yet justify the penitent sinner who believes in Jesus.

This ultimate showing, this final setting forth, for which the old Mosaic system had made such preparation and had so well illustrated its standard terms and ideas, was to be made by bringing forth Christ as being himself the redemption and the propitiation, available through faith in His blood, which should make manifest that God was righteous in the remitting of past sins. Jesus came to fulfill the significance, long almost unknown, of those Old Testament terms "redemption," "Propitiation," "remission of sins."

5. Finally, the vital point (as said already) was to vindicate God's justice in the pardon of sin, to show how He could be just and could yet account as just and also cause to be really just, the sinner who believes in Jesus.

Romans 3:27—*Where is boasting then? It is excluded. By what law? of works? Nay; but by the law of faith.*

Romans 3: 28—*Therefore we conclude that a man is justified by faith without the deeds of the law.*

Is there anything here for the boasting Pharisee who "thanks God that he is not as other men are?" Not a thing: All such boasting is shut off utterly. On what principle? Is it on the principle of the law of works? By no means; but of the law of faith. For, faith puts him right before God on the ground, not of his own meritorious works, but on the ground of his faith in Christ. According to the notion of the proud Pharisee, his deeds were a valid foundation for boasting; but no one could think of boasting over the undeserved mercy that comes to the sinner from Christ through faith in His blood.

The approved text (first clause of verse 28), reads—not "therefore," but "for." We come logically to the conclusion that a man is justified apart from deeds of law, meritorious works having no part in the transaction, constituting no part of the ground of his pardon.*

---

*Cowles, Henry, *The Longer Epistles of Paul*, New York: D. Appleton & Company, 1880, pages 36-39.

Romans 3:31

Romans 3:31—*Do we then make void the law through faith? God forbid: yea, we establish the law.*

Do we then make void law through this faith; literally (the Greek article) through *the* faith of the gospel system? By no means; but we establish law.

Twice in this connection (Romans 3:21, 28) Paul has said very emphatically that this justification by faith takes effect apart from law.

Hence, well aware of the rising thought of his Pharisaic reader, Paul anticipates his reader's objection: "*That* must annul (make void) all law. You save people without law: What is that but abrogating law; making law amount to nothing at all!" "Nay," replies Paul, "we rather establish law on firmer, better ground than ever."

Here two main questions arise: (1) As to the sense of the word "law" in this passage? (2) As to the verification of Paul's words—the manner in which the doctrine of justification by faith only and quite apart from meritorious works, sustains law and makes it firm.

The sense of the word "law" in this passage is in dispute among very worthy critics. Stuart and Meyer argue strenuously that "law" here means the Old Testament scriptures and insist that the next chapter is Paul's vindication of the point put here, showing that the Old Testament Scriptures teach and sustain his doctrine of justification by faith.

I am compelled to dissent from their exegesis, and maintain that "law" here is used in the same sense as above, particularly in Romans 3:21, 28, as "the moral law of God as a rule of duty." I dissent on these grounds:

1. Our authorized version does not fairly represent Paul's word. Paul did not say "the law," but simple "law," without the article. If he had referred to the Old Testament Scriptures, he should have said "*the law*," this being the invariable usage. [[See Matthew 5:17, 18 and 7:12 and 11:13 and 12:5 and so on everywhere if the meaning be—"the law" used for the Old Testament Scriptures.]] But inasmuch as Paul actually said only "law," we are compelled to take the word to mean, "God's great rule of moral duty;" and the more so because the foregoing context and the argument Paul is

making demand it. Certainly, Paul has been speaking of "law" in this very sense in verse 20, "By deeds of law shall no flesh be justified;" "for by law is the better knowledge of sin;" and in verse 21, "But now, *without law* (not without "*the* law"), the righteousness of God is manifested, being witnessed by *the* law and the prophets"—the article being here because in this case it means the Pentateuch—a part of the Old Testament. Also in verse 28, "A man is justified by faith without deeds of law" (not "of *the* law").[[Paul's usage-omitting the article before "law" when he takes the word in its general sense of the rule of duty is entirely uniform.]]

2. Some of the critics say that if we understand Paul to speak of moral law in general, he does not answer the objector at all. To this it should suffice to reply: (a) That he has already said the law is good to give a better knowledge of sin (verse 20), which assumes the law to be in force, not abrogated, but confirmed; and (b) That he defers the further answer to this Pharisaic objection to a later point in his discussion (chapters 6-8).

3. The objection raised here by the Pharisee is certainly not answered in chapter 4, and therefore "law" cannot be used here in the sense of the Old Testament Scriptures as brought forward in that chapter. For, the scope of Romans 4 is *not* aimed to show that Paul's justification by faith established law (in the sense of the Old Testament Scriptures) but that the Old Testament Scriptures establish *it*—not that justification does not make void the Old Testament Scriptures, but that those scriptures do not make void but really prove *it*. That is, Paul appeals to the Old Testament to confirm from them his doctrine of justification by faith, and not at all to refute the Pharisaic objection that he was annulling the law and making it of no account.*

---

*Cowles, Henry, *The Longer Epistles of Paul*, New York: D. Appleton & Company, 1880, pages 40-42.

Romans 4:1-5

The Pharisaic Jew gloried in having Abraham for his father ("We have Abraham for our father," Matthew 3, 9), and assumed himself entitled to every blessing promised to Abraham inasmuch as circumcision brought him within the Abrahamic covenant. Furthermore, it is clear that in his view Abraham and all the circumcised held their blessings on the ground of works, not of faith; of doings, and not of simple believing. Paul knew perfectly how this matter lay in their mind, and therefore devoted this chapter to meet and refute their errors on this point; aiming comprehensively to show that according to their own scriptures Abraham's righteousness (acceptance before God) came of faith, not of works: that David taught the same when he spoke of the blessedness of the man forgiven of sin; that Abraham attained this righteousness of faith *before* he was circumcised, and therefore his righteousness could not depend on his circumcision; that hence he became the father of all believing Gentiles who like himself believed before, and without the aid of, circumcision. As to the circumcised Jew, he could be the father of those only who had like faith with his. This faith of Abraham he sets forth in its constituent elements, particularly showing that it turns, not at all upon works of merit, but wholly upon free grace.

Romans 4:1—*What shall we say then that Abraham our father as pertaining to the flesh, hath found?*
Romans 4: 2—*For if Abraham were justified by works, he hath* whereof *to glory; but not before God.*

Breaking in with apparent abruptness because the notions of the Pharisaic Jews were too well known both to himself and to his readers to require formal statement, Paul asks, "What blessings did our common father derive from his circumcision in the flesh?" The authorized version connects the word "flesh" with "father"; but it is better to connect it with the verb "found": (1) Because there was not the least occasion to say father as to the flesh; and (2) the gist of the question is "What benefit did he derive from fleshly circumcision; that is, from circumcision as an external rite in the flesh?" It is precisely in this sense of the question that Paul proceeds to say. "For if this circumcision, considered as a work, a thing of personal merit, availed to Abraham's justification before God, then he had something to glory in, some ground of personal complacen-

197

cy and even of boasting: but the very idea of this *as toward God* is abhorrent to our moral sense. Therefore, Paul makes this emphatic declaration: How much soever of merit might lie in Abraham's prompt obedience to a painful rite, we can never think of its being the meritorious ground of his salvation *before God!* All boasting in it is excluded in the presence of the great and holy God!

Romans 4:3—*For what saith the Scripture? Abraham believed God, and it was counted unto him for righteousness.*

With the Pharasaic Jew, arguments from his own scriptures are always in order; therefore, Paul appeals to that pivotal passage, the bearing of which on the point in hand was at once entirely plain and perfectly decisive: "Abraham believed God, and it (this faith) was counted unto him for righteousness" (Genesis 15:6). It availed for him unto the result (so the Greek) of righteousness; of acceptance before God as a righteous man.

Romans 4: 4—*Now to him that worketh is the reward not reckoned of grace, but of debt.*
Romans 4: 5—*But to him that worketh not, but believeth on him that justifieth the ungodly, his faith is counted for righteousness.*

The man who works has his reward, not as a gratuity but as a debt. The man who does not work but only believes upon one who justifies the sinner is on a totally different footing. His faith (not his work) is made the ground of his acceptance as righteous. These points are put by Paul very distinctly and in this antithetic form: To the working man his reward does not come by gratuitous mercy, but by right, a debt due; but, on the other hand, to him who worketh not, but simply rests in faith upon Him who justifies the ungodly, his resting faith counts to him for righteousness.*

---

*Cowles, Henry, *The Longer Epistles of Paul*, New York: D. Appleton & Company, 1880, pages 42-44.

Romans 4:16-21

Romans 4:16—*Therefore it is of faith, that it might be by grace; to the end the promise might be sure to all the seed; not to that only which is of the law, but to that also which is of the faith of Abraham; who is the father of us all.*

Romans 4:17—*As it is written, I have made thee a father of many nations, before him whom he believed, even God, who quickeneth the dead, and calleth those things which be not as though they were:*

Romans 4:18—*Who against hope believed in hope, that he might become the father of many nations, according to that which was spoken, So shall thy seed be.*

On this account did God hinge His plan for human salvation upon faith to the end it might be of grace—might afford unlimited scope for His mercy; so that His promise might be firm to all the seed of Abraham (as above in verses 11 and 12); to the Gentile who is Abraham's son only in the matter of faith; and to the Jew who walks in the steps of his lineal father's faith. Put in the phrase of verse 16, it is thus: "Not only to him of the law (the Jew), but to him of Abraham's faith (the Gentile believer)." Now Paul expatiates upon this precious fact that God made Abraham the father of all who like him believe; and thus to the extent of many nations, Gentile as well as Jew.

To set forth the strength of this faith of Abraham in full light, Paul reminds us that Abraham believed in God's power to vivify what was dead, and to speak of things apparently impossible as though they were certain and sure. Thus, in the strength of his faith, Abraham believed against all human probability ("against hope, believed in hope"); and so reached the exalted honor of becoming the father of many nations.

Romans 4:19—*And being not weak in faith, he considered not his own body now dead, when he was about a hundred years old, neither yet the deadness of Sarah's womb;*

Romans 4:20—*He staggered not at the promise of God through unbelief; but was strong in faith, giving glory to God.*

Romans 4:21—*And being fully persuaded that what he had promised, he was able to perform.*

These verses expatiate upon and reaffirm the great faith of this glorious model of implicit confidence in God.*

---

*Cowles, Henry, *The Longer Epistles of Paul*, New York: D. Appleton & Company, 1880, pages 46-47.

Romans 5:8

Romans 5:8—*But God commendeth his love toward us, in that, while we were yet sinners, Christ died for us.*

These facts in the gospel reveal God's wondrous love for us and quicken our responsive love to Him. These facts are brought out here to verify what Paul has been saying, and are therefore introduced by "for" (Greek: "gar"). What he has said of our "peace with God;" of our "access by faith into" this precious state of grace; of the reason we have for even "glorying in tribulation," must be most true *for* while we were yet helpless, power-less, utterly hopeless of self-recovery, in due time Christ died for us sin-ners. This was indeed a marvellous thing, *"for"* (verse 7) scarcely would any one die for a man merely righteous, though for the really *good* man, possibly one might dare to die. But God sets forth His love in strong relief, we might even say He *glorifies* it, inasmuch as, while we were yet sinners, Christ died for us. Infinitely far from being good—far even from being just—indeed being positively wicked rebels—even then Christ laid down His life for us. There were representative men around His very cross gnashing their teeth upon Him in rage and taunting Him with insults while He was meekly enduring those awful agonies and pouring forth His very heart's blood unto death for the guilty.*

---

*Cowles, Henry, *The Longer Epistles of Paul*, New York: D. Appleton & Company, 1880, page 50.

Romans 6:5-7

Romans 6:5—*For if we have been planted together in the likeness of his death, we shall be also in the likeness of his resurrection:*
Romans 6:6—*Knowing this, that our old man is crucified with him, that the body of sin might be destroyed, that henceforth we should not serve sin.*
Romans 6:7—*For he that is dead is freed from sin.*

A new phase of the great analogy appears here, *the planting of seed in the ground*; its undergoing decomposition there; but, as the result, re-appearing in fruitage and glory. Perhaps Paul had in mind those words of his Master: "Except a corn of wheat fall into the ground and die, it abideth alone; but if it die it bringeth forth much fruit" (John 12:24). So Paul thinks of Christ's people as being seed planted in the ground like Christ in His grave, and then, like Him, springing up in the glory of a resurrection to noblest fruitage. "Knowing this" calls special attention to the point to be introduced. Ye ought to understand this well—that our old man of sin must needs be thoroughly crucified as Christ was on His cross, that the old sin-body may be destroyed—put utterly out of the way—so that henceforth we may serve sin no more. All the old propensities—proclivities toward sensual, sinful indulgence—must be slain.

In verse 6, we have a Greek word for "freed" (dikaioo), often used in the sense of "justified," but here in the somewhat peculiar sense—set free, acquitted, absolved, made quit of sin. Then under Paul's figure, it is the dead man who is thus set free from sin, for he has passed out of the earthly sphere—out of the range of worldly influences, considerations, temptations. Happy man! To be thus emancipated from bondage to flesh! If his voluntary spiritual death has made him a free man, thoroughly dead to the powers that impel toward sin, and also alive to all the nobler impulses heavenward, how greatly should he rejoice! In verse 18, Paul uses for the same sense the common word for emancipate—"Being emancipated from sin, ye become servants unto righteousness."*

---

*Cowles, Henry, *The Longer Epistles of Paul*, New York: D. Appleton & Company, 1880, pages 65-66.

Romans 6:11-14

Romans 6:11—*Likewise reckon ye also yourselves to be dead indeed unto sin, but alive unto God through Jesus Christ our Lord.*

The reader should notice carefully that this Christian dying and living, being of the moral sort [not physical] are determined, not by any law of nature and necessity, but by their thinking, "reckoning," willing—by their accounting it so. It is wholly a matter of their free purpose and choice—in this respect entirely unlike physical death and life which in no wise turn upon our own accounting, "reckoning" ourselves to be dead or living. If this distinction is thoroughly considered and understood, the Apostle's meaning will appear clear and pertinent.

Romans 6:12—*Let not sin therefore reign in your mortal body, that ye should obey it in the lusts thereof.*
Romans 6:13—*Neither yield ye your members as instruments of unrighteousness unto sin: but yield yourselves unto God, as those that are alive from the dead, and your members as instruments of righteousness unto God.*

These verses are a logical inference from the verse preceding. Death and life, in this spiritual sense, belong to the voluntary activities of your soul. It is for you to say that sin shall not reign in your mortal body, compelling you to obey it and its damning lusts. Ye must not let it reign! Neither surrender your bodily powers to become the instruments of sin; but consecrate them to God as people made alive unto God from your old death in sin. Ye have said—I am to live to God forevermore! This means —I am to be the slave of sin no more; I am no more to let my powers of either body or mind become instruments of unrighteousness, but only and wholly, to be instruments of righteousness unto the service of God.

Here the reader will notice that thus far in this chapter Paul is answering the question of verse 1: "Shall we continue in sin that grace may abound?" And he answers it by saying, "No! Never! For we are dead to sin!" As Christians, we are committed against sin by the most sacred vows and obligations. We are dead by our voluntary renunciation to all its seductions, fascinations, attractions; and we live unto God with our utmost strength of moral purpose. How then can we allow ourselves to sin? In verse 2, Paul uses a special relative [for "we *that*"] in this pregnant sense: we *being such as* have died to sin—inasmuch as, by our solemn profession, we have renounced sin forever: how shall such men live any longer in sin?

Romans 6:14—*For sin shall not have dominion over you: for ye are not under the law, but under grace.*

Closely connecting this verse with the preceding. Paul seems to say logically—You are free to give your powers unto God, for sin will [future] —will not lord it over you any longer (this should not be expected); sin will no more play the tyrant over you, because you are not under law but under grace. But what does this mean? In what sense of *law* can it be said, "Ye are not under law?" By what logic does it follow that sin shall not tyrannize over people because they are not under law but under grace ?

Briefly, in the Pharisaic sense of "*law*" and of being "under law." Paul is reasoning with Pharisaic Jews. They were men of "*the law*." The old Mosaic law, somewhat badly abused and over-loaded with their traditionary interpretations and appendages, was their recognized rule of life. Obedience to it in their sense of obedience was the ground of their confidence in God's favor. They used the law (in their way) for sanctification and justification. By the law they would become holy men; by the law they assumed they should be accepted before God as righteous and inherit eternal life. They were *under law* therefore for both these great ends.

Paul is no longer a Pharisee. He does not believe in being "under law" in their sense for either sanctification or justification. He has no faith in law (in the Pharisaic sense) as a power either to save people from their sins, or to justify them before God. As a power to save human souls from sin, he looks to grace, not to law. As a ground of justification before God, he holds to faith in Christ and not to legal righteousness.*

---

*Cowles, Henry, *The Longer Epistles of Paul*, New York: D. Appleton & Company, 1880, pages 67-68.

Romans 6:18-23

Romans 6:18—*Being then made free from sin, ye became the servants of righteousness.*

As already suggested in verse 7, "free from sin" is used here in the sense of real emancipation by victory over sin through grace. This being gained, it only remains that we become the willing, free-hearted servants of righteousness.

Romans 6:19—*I speak after the manner of men because of the infirmity of your flesh: for as ye have yielded your members servants to uncleanness and to iniquity unto iniquity; even so now yield your members servants to righteousness unto holiness.*
Romans 6:20—*For when ye were the servants of sin, ye were free from righteousness.*
Romans 6:21—*What fruit had ye then in those things whereof ye are now ashamed? for the end of those things is death.*

This "speaking after the manner of men" seems to mean a method of obvious illustration, easily understood.

As they have been slaves to all uncleanness and to abounding growing iniquity, so now let them consecrate their powers to righteousness, unto the result of real holiness, for so long as they were bond-slaves of sin, they were entirely void of righteousness—had none of it.

What was the fruit of such a life, full of deeds they ought never to think of without shame? Alas! The end of such a course is only death!

Romans 6:22—*But now being made free from sin, and become servants to God, ye have your fruit unto holiness, and the end everlasting life.*
Romans 6:23—*For the wages of sin is death; but the gift of God as eternal life trough Jesus Christ our Lord.*

This contrast is at once clear and full of force. The legitimate fruit of holy living—everlasting life; but the wages of sin, death only, death wholly, death eternally and in character, most appalling!

The free gift of God's grace to those who live righteously, eternal life— over against that awful, everlasting death ?*

---

*Cowles, Henry, *The Longer Epistles of Paul*, New York: D. Appleton & Company, 1880, pages 70-71.

Henry Cowles

(Served Oberlin College: 1835-1881)

A.B., Yale University, 1826; graduated Yale Seminary, 1828; D.D. Hillsdale College, 1863.

Oberlin College: Professor of Languages, 1835-37; Professor of Ecclesiastical History and Pastoral Theology, 1837-40; Professor of the Literature of the Old Testament, 1840-48; Member of the Prudential Committee, 1836-37 and 1843-81; Member of Board of Trustees, 1851-81; General Agent, 1860-63; Lecturer on Prophecy and Biblical Introduction, 1869-78. Died Janesville, Wisconsin, September 6, 1881.

Charles Grandison Finney

(Served Oberlin College: 1835-1875)

Oberlin College: Professor of Systematic Theology, 1835-58; Professor of Pastoral Theology, 1835-75; Member of Board of Trustees, 1846-51; Elected President of Oberlin College, August 26, 1851; President and *ex officio* Member Board of Trustees, 1851-65; Died Oberlin, Ohio, August 16, 1875.

From *General Catalogue of Oberlin College Seventy-Fifth Anniversary*, 1833-1908. Oberlin, Ohio, April 1, 1909, pages Int. 139, Int. 146.

About Agion Press

Agion Press began in November 2005, with the publication of the limited, numbered, and signed edition of *Principles of Righteousness* by Charles G. Finney. Agion Press expands and improves the new "Finney's Principles Series" by compiling Finney's Lessons according to the books of the Bible. Newly edited for today's readers, the new "Finney's Principles Series" gives students of Finney improved textual uniformity while conforming to Finney's meaning. To help readers focus on many of the key thoughts in Finney's lectures and sermons, the books in the new "Finney's Principles Series" include Study Questions for individuals and groups. A commentary by Henry Cowles or other commentators on the key verses in Finney's Lessons will be found in the back of each book. Henry Cowles served as a Professor of Oberlin College and as Editor of the "Oberlin Evangelist," the college newspaper that printed many of Finney's sermons. Go to FinneysPrinciples.com for additional free resources and study guides.

Agion Press derives the name from the New Testament Greek word "agion," which means "to make holy." Agion Press books will teach the truth in love to help people walk in holiness with Jesus Christ as their Lord and Savior. Charles Finney often affirmed this scriptural truth: "Make every effort to live in peace with all men and to be holy; without holiness no one will see the Lord" (Hebrews 12:14). Regarding Jesus Christ, Agion Press affirms: "Salvation is found in no one else, for there is no other name under heaven given to men by which we must be saved" (Acts 4:12). All Agion Press books uphold the truth that "All Scripture is God-breathed and is useful for teaching, rebuking, correcting and training in righteousness, so that the man of God may be thoroughly equipped for every good work" (2 Timothy 3:16, 17).

Visit the Agion Press website regularly to learn more about additional, new Agion Press releases. Feel free to contact us with your suggestions or questions.

Agion Press
P.O. Box 1052
Edmond, Oklahoma 73083-1052
AgionPress.com

Printed in the United States
120173LV00009B/262-267/A